Florida Bounty

A Celebration of Florida Cuisine and Culture

Eric R. Jacobs & Sandra M. Jacobs

Pineapple Press, Inc.
Sarasota, Florida

Inquiries should be addressed to:

Pineapple Press, Inc.
P.O. Box 3889
Sarasota, Florida 34230

www.pineapplepress.com

Library of Congress Cataloging-in-Publication Data

Jacobs, Eric R., 1972-
  Florida bounty : a celebration of Florida cuisine and culture / Eric R. Jacobs &
Sandra M. Jacobs.— 1st ed.
     p. cm.
  ISBN-13: 978-1-56164-352-3 (pbk. : alk. paper)
  ISBN-10: 1-56164-352-1 (pbk. : alk. paper)
   1. Cookery, American. 2. Cookery—Florida. I. Jacobs, Sandra M., 1976- II. Title.
  TX715.J2165 2006
  641.59759—dc22

                                                                    2005033056

First Edition
10 9 8 7 6 5 4 3 2 1

Design by Shé Heaton
Printed in the United States of America

For Mom

Contents

Introduction   1

Regional Florida Menus

A Florida Thanksgiving   4
The Tampa Special   6
Boating Picnic   7
Football Tailgate Party   8
Panhandle Fry Fest   10
A Capitol Brunch   11
Miami High Life   12
Key West Fiesta   13

Florida Ingredients

Citrus Fruits   16
Other Fruits   16
Fish   17
Herbs and Spices   18
Meats   19
Seafood—Shellfish and Bivalves   19
Vegetables   20
Peppers   21
Other   21

Drinks

Southern Sweet Tea   23
Cool Lemonade   24
Café con Leche   24
Fruit Smoothies   25

Jubilant Orange Creams   26
Strawberry Daiquiri   26
Perfect Planter's Punch   27
Mojo Mojito   27
Cuba Libre   28
Spring Hill Bloody Mary   29
Piña Colada   30
Beach Margarita   31

Appetizers

Tangy Florida Seafood Dip   33
Original Heart of Palm Dip   34
Heart of Palm Cocktail   36
Mussels with Citrus Beurre Blanc   37
Oysters on the Half Shell   39
Big Money Oysters Rockefeller   40
Crabby Stuffed Mushrooms   42
Gulf Coast Ceviche   44
Florida Citrus Salsa   46

Salads

Tarpon Springs Greek Salad   48
Chilly Dilly Shrimps a.k.a. "Shrimps à la Sergio"   50
Papaya, Tomato, and Cilantro Salad   51
Classic Caesar Salad   52
Florida Lobster and Blue Crab Salad in Avocado   54

Soups

Blue Crab Bisque   56
Tampa Garbanzo Bean Soup   57
Oyster Stew   58
Gator Black Bean Chili   59
Vidalia (French-style) Onion Soup   60

Sandwiches

Spicy Shrimp Po' Boy   62
Soft-shell Crab Po' Boy   63
Florida Blackened Grouper Sandwich   64
Tampa-style Cuban Sandwich   66

Entrées

Stone Crab Claws   68
Blue Crab Fest   69
Grouper with Orange Sauce   70
Costa Rican–style Grouper al Ajillo   71
Salted Red Snapper   72
Pasta with Florida Shellfish in Tomato Cream   74
Linguini with Classic Clam Sauce   76
Pop's Red Clam Sauce   78
Key West Pork Tenderloin   79
Pan-fried Soft-shell Crab with Homemade Cole Slaw   80
Florida Lobster Ravioli in Sage Butter   82
Maryland-style Crab Cakes   84
Dixie Fried Fish   85

Florida Jambalaya with Grits   86
Shrimp Scampi Pizza   88
Grecian Urn Burger   90
Caribbean-style Beef and Sugar Cane
          Stew in Coconut Milk   92
24-Hour Yogurt-marinated Beef Roast   94
Super Fast, Super Good Turkey   95
Stuffed Tomatoes   96

Sides

Grits, grits, grits!   98
Fried Green Tomatoes   101
Orange Hush Puppies   102
Conch Fritters   103
Thanksgiving Blue Crab Stuffing   105
Fresh Mango Salsa   106

Breakfast Specialties

Fancy Blue Crab Quiche   108
Luscious Shrimp Omelet with Spinach & Cream Cheese   109
Buttermilk Pancakes with
          Blueberries & Maple Syrup   110
French Toast with Fresh Strawberries and Bananas   111
Mom's Banana Bread   112

Sweet Things

Classic Key Lime Pie   114
Key Lime Cheesecake   115
Fast and Fancy Angel Food Cake
        with Chocolate and Strawberry Sauce   117
Tres Leches (Three Milk Cake)   118
Tallahassee Lassie Pecan Tassies   119
Tangy Lemon Bars   120
Southern-style Pecan Pralines   121
Blackberry Tart   122
Mamma Guava Pastry   124

Condiments

All-the-Time Mustard Yogurt Sauce   126
Voodoo Sauce   127
Kickin' Cocktail Sauce   129

Index   131

Introduction

T his book is dedicated to the state of Florida and all those who have helped to make it the wonderful paradise it is. Florida is not just a place of warm winters and pristine beaches, but also the site of wondrous cuisine. We have written this cookbook based on our own passions for food and beverage. It is a cornucopia of experiences throughout the state, as well as our experiences abroad, which we've adapted to the Florida climate and the variety of fresh ingredients available. There are original recipes, recipes inspired by meals we have had throughout the world, as well southern coastal classics with new and intriguing adaptations. Florida is a place of colorful landscape, climate, history—and a colorful plate.

Florida cuisine has many contributors, including the original Native American Indians; the early Spanish, French, and English settlers from the sixteenth through the nineteenth centuries; Cuban immigrants in the nineteenth and twentieth centuries; retirees and warmth-seeking snowbirds of the American North; and the Caribbean and Latin immigrants of the twentieth and twenty-first centuries. And let's not forget today's new residents and visitors from all over the world. These groups and the many flavors they have brought to Florida provide a plentiful and delicious bounty of Florida foods.

Florida is known the world over for beautiful weather, theme parks, and oranges. But Florida is also about food. Running down the Gulf coast from Pensacola to Key West, then up the Atlantic coast to Jacksonville—Florida's long shoreline offers a bounty of seafood. All the state in between is filled with locally grown fruits and vegetables. No wonder Florida natives and visitors like to eat, and eat well.

We have attempted to create a feel for and taste of Florida, whether you are celebrating the warm green spring, lounging in the long hot summer, battening down for the fall hurricane season, or enjoying the relatively brief coolness of winter. Florida food, like the cuisine of many places, is modified by the seasons, though the degree of seasonality decreases as you move down the peninsula. Therefore the changes are subtler the farther south you go. Tallahassee has four distinct seasons, and therefore different foods for each, while Miami enjoys a year-round bounty of tropical delicacies.

Through this book we hope to share not only food and beverages, but also ways to bring dishes and drinks together in a special harmony. We hope to inspire you to travel to some of the places in which we have found our muse. There are many such locations in Florida, ranging from world-famous steak houses to divey seafood shacks.

While this book is specific to Florida and Floridian ingredients, the modern world allows for many exotic ingredients to be had anywhere you happen to be. Therefore, this is not just a cookbook to be used in and around Florida, but anywhere you are inspired by the spirit of this sunny and warm place. Do not be limited by geography; if you can get many of the ingredients listed here, then you can make any day a Florida day.

༺

Regional
Florida Menus

A Florida Thanksgiving

Big Money Oysters
Rockefeller, p. 40
Tangy Florida Seafood Dip,
p. 33
Crabby Stuffed Mushrooms,
p. 42
Stone Crab Claws with All-
the-Time Mustard Yogurt
Sauce, p. 68 and 126
Grouper in Orange Sauce,
p. 70

Super Fast, Super Good
Turkey, p. 95
Thanksgiving Blue Crab
Stuffing, p. 105
Tallahassee Lassie Pecan
Tassies, p. 119
Classic Key Lime Pie, p. 114

The American Thanksgiving holiday began as a celebration of
the local harvest, bounty, and
friendship. Native Americans
brought the natural indigenous
bounty to be shared with the
newly introduced foods of the
recently arrived Europeans. In
St. Augustine, the Spanish
explorers enjoyed the local
bounty with Native Americans.
With this same spirit in modern
times, Floridians celebrate a Florida
Thanksgiving.

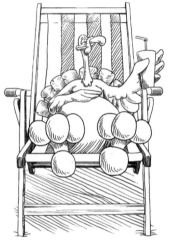

Seafood is part of the Florida bounty, as are fruits, vegetables, nuts, and yes, even turkey. A delightful and seasonal
bounty can be introduced with a serving of luxurious oysters
Rockefeller, their rich creaminess perfect in the cooler
November air. If your meal will be later in the day, a hearty
tangy Florida seafood dip will keep all the guests happy waiting for the big meal. Crabby stuffed mushrooms are such a
classic in our family that Thanksgiving would be called off

without them. Stone crabs will be enjoyed regardless of the setting, guests, or accompanying dishes. Take caution, however, as once you serve them their presence will be expected annually. No holiday tradition has ever been adopted so fast.

When in season, grouper is the First Fish of Florida, so what could be a better choice on such a food-focused holiday? Served with a fresh orange sauce (the first sweet oranges should be coming available in November), you will have a wonderful match for the many accompanying dishes. While farm-raised turkey is the most common staple at holiday tables in all states of the country, wild turkey can be found in Florida and is thus a true part of the local bounty. It can be roasted quickly to a dark caramel brown, fried, or slow-roasted for twelve hours to pale golden perfection. Whichever way you prepare your turkey, go for it!

Blue crab stuffing brings the bounty of the sea back to the table. The crab is a delectable match to the rich meat of turkey, as well as a mellow contrast to the tangy tenderness of the grouper in orange sauce.

For dessert, Tallahassee lassie pecan tassies bring out the tastes of the Old South. These tartlets are more common in the north of Florida, but wherever you serve them, your guests will have positive and delightful things to say about these gooey little treats. You might also try the classic Key lime pie, whose tartness will match the bounty of seafood.

We hope this menu gives you a few new ideas for that "foodiest" of all holidays. Continue to serve your favorites as well, and remember: it is Thanksgiving, and not all the dishes are supposed to go together anyway (especially Aunt Vera's creamed corn!).

The Tampa Special

Mojo Mojitos, p. 27
Tampa-style Cuban
    Sandwiches, p. 66
Tampa Garbanzo Bean Soup,
    p. 57

Costa Rican–style Grouper al
    Ajillo, p. 71
Tres Leches, p. 118
Café con Leche, p. 24

Tampa is an industrial city situated on the waters of Tampa Bay, the nation's second largest bay. The food is a mixture of the local bounty of the sea and other influences, including a strong Cuban community. Ybor City, Tampa's bustling entertainment district, is the historic center of the immigrant culture. Founded by a Cuban businessman as a place to produce cigars (at one point Ybor City was the world's largest cigar producer), the culinary influence has spread throughout central Florida and beyond. To share in this historic taste of Ybor City and Tampa you need only to produce this simple but delicious meal.

With their bittersweet flavor, mojo mojitos will stimulate everyone's appetites. For finger food, serve Cuban sandwiches, which are widely considered a Tampa invention and make a delectable dish. A perfect combination with a Cuban sandwich is a bowl of luscious garbanzo bean soup, perfect for dipping any extra Cuban bread.

With appetites entertained but wanting more, serve a large plate of grouper al ajillo. The firm white meat of the grouper works perfectly with the sweet tastes of the oven-roasted garlic. This dish is light enough to serve with a sandwich and rich bowl of soup for lunch or dinner.

Tres leches is a wonderfully rich and sweet dessert to follow all the savory flavors of a Tampa-style Cuban meal. If all of this makes you a bit sleepy, try a little sugar and caffeine boost to finish off the meal. No meal is complete without the thick, sweet Cuban-style coffee known as café con leche. While more common in the morning, the sweetness from the canned milk is a natural match for the tres leches, and a perfect end to this typical Tampa meal.

Boating Picnic

Gulf Coast Ceviche, p. 44   Strawberries and Whipped
Chilly Dilly Shrimps, p. 50   Cream
Florida Blackened Grouper   Cool Lemonade, p. 24
    Sandwiches, p. 64

Water, sun, fun, family, friends, and good food are the essentials to a wondrous day on the boat (a back porch will do if a boat cannot be found). It is easy to work up an appetite while spending a full day either fishing for your dinner or just soaking up the Florida sunshine on a boat. A mid-afternoon feast that focuses on fruits of the sea and fresh flavors will elevate an all-day offshore excursion from a nice time to an everlasting memory.

Seafood ceviche highlights "frutti di mare" in its purest form. Rather than cooking the seafood over high heat or frying it, which might hide the flavors, the dish serves as a channel for experiencing the true flavors of the food, augmented only with herbs and citrus.

Chilly dilly shrimps are refreshing and even invigorating when served cold out of the icebox, and like ceviche, can be made the day before, thus requiring minimal effort on the boat, where space is often limited. Blackened grouper sandwiches will require the use of a broiler, stovetop, or grill, but are most satisfying and provide a spice that blends perfectly with the salty air of the ocean.

Finally, berries and cream create a simple, refreshing finale to a meal that would please even Neptune. Don't forget the sunscreen!

❧

Football Tailgate Party

Soft-shell Crab Po' Boys,
  p. 63
Spicy Shrimp Po' Boys, p. 62
Florida Citrus Salsa and
  Tortilla Chips, p. 46

Tarpon Springs Greek Salad,
  p. 48
Tangy Lemon Bars, p. 120

Football is not a sport in Florida— it's a religion. From peewee to the pros, football is the king of sports. Coming in a close second to the game itself is the tailgate party, which can occur both before and after the game. The food and beverages provided set the mood for the state and country's most popular sport. While tailgating is not a Florida exclusive, it can be made unique if you use the local bounty. We have included a few ideas that keep well and are easily

made in large quantities, for football makes everyone hungry.
Po' boys are perfect for the festive atmosphere of a tailgate party. The shrimp and soft shell crabs are decadent and
will be enjoyed by all. The thick bread can also provide a nice
buffer for your stomach, just in case a few alcoholic beverages
are consumed during the day. Citrus salsa is the truest Florida
dip, as all of its ingredients grow in the state. Besides, what is
any festive outdoor event without some interpretation of
chips and dip? Also a must for any outdoor event is salad. The
Tarpon Springs Greek salad offers a little something for everyone: hearty potato salad for some and a lighter bite for others
(you can trade your potato salad for an extra tomato slice or
Kalamata olive). It is the perfect refreshing taste after a thick
and spicy po' boy. Greek salad also stands up better to warmer
temperatures in the early fall than many other salads.

And don't forget the dessert! For a little sweetness on
your walk to the stadium, lemon bars are hard to beat. They
are great on a hot afternoon with a cool beverage and equally
as tasty on cold evenings with coffee and other hot beverages.
And remember, tailgating does not have to be limited to football, so why not make an event of your next soccer game,
horse race, or bowling match?

⚭

Panhandle Fry Fest

Oysters on the Half Shell,
p. 39
Conch Fritters, p. 103
Dixie Fried Fish, p. 85
Orange Hush Puppies, p. 102

Florida Jambalaya with Grits,
p. 86
Sliced Watermelon
Southern Sweet Tea, p. 23

Over the last century, many ambitious politicians in the state of Florida have kicked off their campaigns with a good, old-fashioned fry fest. Indeed, very few Florida Panhandle natives would be able to recall a childhood without them. "Back in the day" memories are conjured easily of large barrel drums filled with hot oil over an open flame, waiting to fry catfish, mouthwatering hush puppies and conch fritters, to be washed down with an iced tea so sweet that your dentist, who was there to support the campaign, cringed with every sip taken. Raw oysters were shucked by the dozen and slurped down even faster, sometimes solo and sometimes with a saltine and hot sauce. Seafood jambalaya is a newer addition, but one that matches perfectly with the Southern traditions and flavors. And one must not forget the glorious watermelon that provides water to your system on hot summer days, a delicious flavor, and most importantly hours of fun for children in seed-spitting contests. Indeed, no political campaign in north Florida is truly complete without the mandatory fry fest!

A Capitol Brunch

Fancy Blue Crab Quiche, p. 108   Blackberry Tart, p. 122

Grapefruit Halves   Freshly Squeezed Orange Juice

Buttermilk Pancakes with   Southern Sweet Tea, p. 23

   Fresh Blueberries, p. 110

Spicy Jalapeño Grits, p. 99

Fried Green Tomatoes, p. 101

Tallahassee is where the government of Florida starts and ends. This somewhat ironic, as Tallahassee is a Southern town in old sense with beautiful canopy roads, majestic oaks, and prosperous pecan trees, which has little in common with the more famous cities of Orlando, Miami, and Tampa. The iced tea is more often sweet than not, and the pace is a bit slower. But Tallahassee is an integral part of Florida, and the social and culinary traditions are fun and delicious. Brunches are a typical Sunday occurrence in Tallahassee, and usually start late in the morning to allow for the proper church-going activities (or sleeping in). While the focus is often on traditional breakfast foods, there are also lunch-based alternatives to account for the time of day.

In this typical Sunday brunch, we have included buttermilk pancakes with fresh blueberries. As blueberries grow well in the Tallahassee climate, these can often be obtained during a Saturday afternoon excursion. Jalapeño grits take a traditional breakfast food and spice them up to complement a more traditional lunch option—fried green tomatoes. A blackberry tart will be delicious with either culinary choice. Fresh squeezed orange juice and the requisite sweet tea round out the meal with a Florida touch. This is best enjoyed with friends or family surrounded by slow, genteel Southern hospitality.

Miami High Life

Classic Caesar Salad, p. 52   *Key Lime Cheesecake, p. 115*
Blue Crab Bisque, p. 56
Stone Crab Claws with All-
    the-Time Mustard Yogurt
    Sauce, p. 68 and 126

Some of the finest eating in Florida's most renowned city is often found in simple elegance. Looking good is a priority in Miami, but eating and drinking well are not far behind. With a handful of distinctive dishes, a Miami event can be a most memorable and tasty experience.

The centerpiece to this bounty is the seasonal stone crabs, both succulent and sweet. Like most great shellfish, stone crabs need very little accompaniment—a bit of melted butter, or perhaps a savory mustard sauce, is all it takes. With these large crustacean grabbers as your centerpiece, you can create an elegant event with a few haute but simple dishes.

Blue crab bisque is luscious and indulgent, almost a celebration in itself. Best served at the beginning of the meal, this rich and creamy soup will awaken your taste buds. Remembering that opposites often attract, a tangy Caesar salad will carry the high-flying party to the moon above. The zesty richness of the lemon and anchovy will only enhance the sweet meats of the stone crabs, simultaneously keeping your palate fresh and ever ready for more.

After such a cornucopia of luxurious tastes your mouth will be ready for a soft sweetness, while not quite ready to give up on the zing. Key lime cheesecake is the perfect answer. The richness of cheesecake is infused with the local tastes of the unique little key lime, for a wonderful conclusion to an elegant meal. Whether you are in South Beach or Coconut Grove, or on your own back porch, these tastes will help you find the true atmosphere of Miami.

⬲

Key West Fiesta

Florida Lobster and Blue Crab
Salad in Avocado, p. 54
Key West Pork Tenderloin
with Mango Salsa, p. 79
Papaya, Tomato, and Cilantro
Salad, p. 51

Classic Key Lime Pie, p. 114
Piña Coladas and
Beach Margaritas,
p. 30 and 31

Having fun and checking out—these are crucial in Key West. The city is arguably the most decadent in the state. If you want to party Key West style, try some of the local bounty and get festive.

Being islands, the Keys are surrounded by all the bounty of Florida's warm tropical waters, but the undeniable pinnacle of that bounty is the Florida spiny lobster. It lacks the big pinchers of its Maine cousin, but its big tail is still the finest of seafood. Lobster and blue crab (the only seafood better than lobster) are perfect matches for the creaminess of a fresh Florida avocado. Serve this up as a cool salad and your festivities will begin with a bang. However, this is not the only salad of the day. A papaya, tomato, and cilantro salad will not let you forget you are in the island tropics. The three primary ingredients form a trifecta of tastes in your mouth, rich and creamy from the papaya, zesty from the tomato, and tangy from the cilantro.

While enjoying these delicious salads and tasty beverages like piña coladas and margaritas (after all, this is Margaritaville), get your pork roast ready for the fire. After cooking the pork loin and devouring the first few bites you will know the joys of Floribbean cuisine, a tantalizing combination of tropical fruits and the scorching smokiness of regional peppers. Fear not though, as the heat of the peppers is moderated by cooking and the sticky sweetness of the mango.

Not quite overwhelmed, you ought to have just enough vigor left to savor the quintessential Florida dessert, Key lime pie. Remember the real thing is yellow with a slight greenish hue, not green, and it is not served with a meringue. As for the discussions about whipped cream, make it part of your party. We do not use whipped cream, but will not ask you not to do so. It's a fiesta, so have all you want and enjoy the mood and spirit that is Key West. ✺

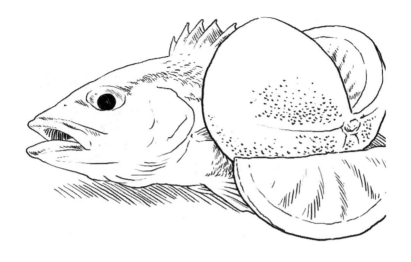

Florida
Ingredients

Citrus Fruits

Grapefruit *(Citrus paradisi):* Large yellow to pink fruit with sweet-sour, juicy pulp

Key lime *(Citrus aurantifolia swingle):* Small yellow-green tart limes native to the Florida Keys

Lemon *(Citrus limon):* Yellow fruit with sour, juicy pulp

Lime *(Citrus aurantifolia):* Green fruit with a tangy, juicy pulp

Orange *(Citrus sinensis):* Orange fruit with sweet, juicy pulp

Other Fruits

Avocado *(Persea americana):* Pear-shaped, green, thin-skinned fruit with rich, creamy flesh and large pit. It has one of the highest fat contents in the fruit family. Skin is not edible.

Banana *(Musa x paradisiaca L.):* Narrow, curved, yellow fruit with a peelable skin and white creamy flesh. Skin is not edible.

Blackberry *(Rubus spp.):* Cluster of tiny purple to black berries with a sweet, tart flavor. Entire fruit is edible.

Blueberry *(Vaccinium spp.):* Small, round, blue to black fruit with purple sweet juice. Entire fruit is edible.

Cantaloupe *(Cucumis melo):* Round melon with a course, textured skin. Light orange flesh with strong fragrance and very sweet flavor, the skin is not edible.

Coconut *(Cocos nucifera L.):* The largest of all nuts, filled with milky water and hard, white, sweet flesh. Husk is not edible.

Guava *(Psidium guajava):* Yellow pear-shaped fruit with a sweet, sticky, pink flesh. Skin is not edible.

Mango *(Mangifera indica):* Yellow to red skin with a stringy, sticky yellow-orange flesh that is very sweet and has a flat center pit. Skin is not edible.

Papaya *(Carica papaya):* Yellow-green fruit shaped like a large pear with mushy, sweet and pale orange meat, strong flavor. Skin is not edible.

Pomegranate *(Punica granatum):* Deep red fruit with hard, paperlike skin. The seeds resemble red corn cornels. The edible juicy flesh encasing the seeds has a bitter raspberry flavor. Skin and flesh around the seeds are not edible.

Star fruit *(Averrha carambola):* Opaque, yellow fruit with mild citrus flavors. Slices are star-shaped. Entire fruit is edible.

Strawberry *(Fragaria* x *ananassa):* Red, heart-shaped fruit with tiny external seeds and a sweet flavor. Entire fruit is edible.

Tomato *(Lycopersicon esculentum* L.): Green, yellow, orange, or more commonly red, heavily seeded fruit with a sweet to savory flavor.

Watermelon *(Citrullus lanatus* var.): Large green fruit with sweet, watery, pink flesh and black, flat seeds. Rind is not edible.

Fish

Amberjack *(Seriola dumerili):* Light, firm fish with delicious mild flavor

Catfish *(Ameiurus catus):* Freshwater bottom feeder with delicate white meat. Served without the skin.

Dolphin, also known as Mahi Mahi *(Coryphaena hippurus):* Light fish with a flaky texture when cooked. Great for fillets or sandwiches.

Gag Grouper *(Mycteroperca microlepis):* Deep-saltwater white-meat fish; served in steaks, fillets, or strips with the skin removed. Mild flavor.

Florida Pompano *(Trachinotus carolinus):* White flesh with mild flavor, usually smaller fillets.

Flounder *(Pleuronectes americanus):* Flat fish with white meat; served in fillets without the skin. Mild flavor.

Mullet *(Mugil curema):* Freshwater or saltwater fish; served in fillets with the skin on. Most commonly prepared smoked. Strong flavor.

Mangrove Snapper *(Lutjanus argentimaculatus):* Shallow-water white-meat fish; served in fillets with the skin on. Similar flavor to Red Snapper.

Red Snapper *(Lutjanus campechanus):* Deep-water white-meat fish; served in fillets with the skin on. Medium flavor.

⮂

Herbs and Spices

Basil *(Ocimum basilicum):* Green leafy herb with a sweet, slightly peppery taste.

Chives *(Allium schoenoprasm):* This long, thin, white and green herb is smallest member of the onion family and has a mild and slightly garlic flavor.

Cilantro *(Coriandrum sativum):* Green soft herb with a pungent, slightly tangy flavor.

Cumin *(Cominum cyminu):* Dried herb common in Caribbean, Mexican, and Eastern Mediterranean cuisines. It has strong pungent aroma and mildly bitter flavor.

Oregano *(Origanum vulgare):* Soft green herb with a medium fresh and slightly minty flavor.

Parsley *(Petroselinum crispum):* Soft green herb available with either flat or curly leaves with a mild celery flavor. All parts of the plant exhibit the same characteristic aroma; it is strongest in the root. Flat leaf is more aromatic and flavorful than curly, which is more common as a garnish.

Rosemary *(Rosemaryinus officinalis):* Deep green, soft, rounded needle-like leaves on hard wood stems. Strongly aromatic (reminiscent of camphor or eucalyptus), resinous, and slightly bitter.

Sage *(Salvia officinallis):* Light green leaves with soft fabric feel. Slightly bitter and aromatic.

Thyme *(Thymus vulgaris):* Small-leaved green herb used a common flavoring agent with a mild, woody flavor.

⮂

Meats

Alligator *(Alligator mississippiensis):* White tail meat, chewy to tough with firm texture and a medium to strong flavor.

Beef *(Bos taurus):* Red meat with soft to firm texture. Mild to moderately strong flavor.

Chicken *(Gallus domesticus):* Medium dark leg meat to very white breast meat and a mild flavor.

Domestic Turkey *(Meleagris gallopavo):* Dark leg meat to white breast meat with mild to slight gamy flavor.

Frog legs *(Rana catesbeiana):* Tender white meat with chicken-like characteristics and a mild to medium flavor.

Pork *(Sus scrofa):* White to pink meat with medium to firm texture and a mild to medium flavor.

Quail *(Coturnix cotumix japonica):* Small game bird with all dark meat and mild gamy flavor.

Wild Turkey *(Meleagris gallopavo):* Large game bird with dark meat and medium to strong gamy flavor.

⟡

Seafood—Shellfish and Bivalves

Bay Scallops *(Aequipecten irradians):* Hinged shelled mollusk with a sweet, white meat

Blue Crab *(Callinectes sapidus):* Eight-legged, two-clawed, blue crustacean with a sweet, white meat. The body and claw meat are edible.

Blue Crab, Soft-shell *(Callinectes sapidus):* Recently molted blue crab with soft outer shell. The entire crab is edible.

Clams *(Mercenaria mercenaria):* Bivalve mollusk with a hard, light, gray shell and chewy meat.

Conch *(Strombus gigas):* A large spiral mollusk with pinkish-white meat.

Florida Spiny Lobster *(Panulirus argus):* Large blue-gray crustacean without the large claws of its famous Northern cousin. The tail has rich, dense, sweet edible meat.

Mussels *(Dreissena polymorpha):* Bivalve mollusk with a black shiny shell and rich, creamy meat.

Oysters *(Crassostrea virginia):* Bivalve mollusk with an irregular gray shell and a sweet metallic flavor.

Shrimp: A variety of species of small, pink, long-tailed crustacean with a firm meat. Common Florida varieties of shrimp include pink, brown, white, and rock shrimp. All varieties of shrimp are sold according to size.

Stone Crab *(Menippe mercenaria):* A red and white crustacean with mildly sweet, white meat. When fished, the largest claw is removed and the live crab is thrown back into the water.

Vegetables

Corn *(Zea mays):* Sweet, yellow or white "ear" vegetable widely available in late summer.

Corn Grits: Coarse-gound dried corn. Common in the American South, grits are typically eaten as a porridge-type food.

Garlic *(Allium sativum):* Pungent, segmented bulb of a perennial plant a member of the Lily family, closely related to the onion.

Hearts of Palm *(Bactris gasipaes):* Inner stalk of the palmetto palm, high in calcium.

Onions *(Allium cepa):* Underground bulb is related to leeks, garlic, and chives and is prized for its distinct, pungent flavor and aroma.

Shallots *(Alium ascalonicum):* Small member of the onion family with a mild fragrance and taste of onion and garlic mixed.

Peppers

Green (Bell) (*Capsicum annum* L): Sweet. Mild.

Red (Bell) (*Capsicum annum* L): Sweet, best when served roasted with the skins removed. Mild.

Yellow (Bell) (*Capsicum annum* L): Sweet. Mild.

Orange (Bell) (*Capsicum annum* L): Sweet and nutty. Mild.

Habanero *(Capsicum chinense):* The hottest of all peppers. Use caution when handling. Super hot.

Banana (*Capsicum annum* L): Long yellow pepper resembling a banana, sweet and great in cooking and for pickling. Mild.

Finger Hot (*Capsicum frutescens* L): Small green to red chili pepper. Hot.

Jalapeño (*Capsicum annum*): Short cigar-shaped pepper with distinctive smoky, herbal flavor. Very hot.

Red Chili *(Capsicum frutescens* L): Small red peppers with delicious smoky flavors. Hot.

Other

Pecans *(Carya illinoensis):* Nut with a dry and pasty texture and an enjoyable flavor.

Sugar Cane *(Saccharum officinarum):* A large tropical grass that can be boiled down into sugar; has a strong sweet flavor.

White Mushrooms *(Agricus bisporus):* Any number of fungi, ranging in color from black to white and in size from that of a bean sprout to a large pancake.

Drinks

Southern Sweet Tea

After years of careful research, we have determined that the southern edge of the "Sweet Tea Line" runs in an east-west direction through Gainesville, Florida. South of Gainesville, sweet tea is the exception, while to the north it is the rule. While this may seem unimportant, it will help to explain the reaction of the waitress when you order sweet tea in Clearwater and get a funny look in return.

2 quarts water
4 tea bags (Lipton black tea
  or similar brand)
1/2 cup sugar
Ice

1 medium lemon, sliced, for
  garnish
Fresh mint for garnish

Bring water to near boil. Add tea bags and remove from heat. Allow tea bags to steep 4 minutes, then remove the tea bags and add sugar. Stir until sugar dissolves and allow the tea to cool to room temperature. Pour over ice and serve with a lemon slice and a sprig of fresh mint. Refrigerate for up to 2 weeks. *Makes 2 quarts of iced tea.*

Note: If hot tea is transferred directly to the refrigerator, the tea will become cloudy.

Cool Lemonade

On a hot summer day there is nothing more refreshing than a tall, cool glass of homemade lemonade. The sweet and tangy taste can quench even the driest thirst. Considering the length of Florida summers, we enjoy the delights of fresh lemonade almost year-round!

1 part granulated sugar	*Ice*
1 part lemon juice, preferably	*1 lemon, sliced, for garnish*
fresh squeezed	
6 parts cold water	

Mix sugar and lemon juice. Add water and stir well. Serve in a tall glass with ice, garnished with a lemon slice and a straw. For a single serving, use a tablespoon for measurement. If making a serving for 8, use a cup for measurement.

☙

Café con Leche

Café con leche and Cuban toast (pressed or toasted Cuban bread with butter) is often a favorite Florida breakfast. This phenomenon is not surprising, considering the large Cuban population found throughout the state. "Coffee with milk" makes a sweet, creamy, and delicious change from typical coffee.

1 12-ounce can evaporated milk
1 1/2 tablespoons granulated sugar
12 ounces strong brewed Cuban coffee (dark French roast can
be substituted)

Heat milk on stovetop over medium-high heat. Add the sugar, stirring constantly. Be sure to spoon off any "skin" that develops on the surface of the milk while heating. Meanwhile, fill coffee cups half full with coffee. When the milk begins to steam, pour into each coffee cup, filling to the top. *Makes 3 8-ounce cups.*

☙

Fruit Smoothies

Delicious as either a healthy breakfast or a refreshing afternoon snack, fruit smoothies can be varied to highlight the seasonal bounty of fruit wherever you may live. Use these recipes as a base, and feel free to substitute fruits and add nutritional supplements such as ginseng, soy, or protein powder. Think of fruit smoothies as your vehicle to better health!

Tropical Smoothie

1 banana, peeled and halved
1/2 mango, peeled and sliced in large pieces
1/4 cup plain low-fat yogurt
1 cup of ice

Berry Smoothie

1/4 pint blueberries   *1/2 cup low-fat milk*
1/4 pint blackberries   *1 cup of ice*
1/2 pint strawberries

For both smoothies, blend all ingredients for 60 seconds in a blender at high speed. Serve with a garnish of fresh mint, if desired. *Both the berry and tropical smoothies make 2 8-ounce servings each.*

Jubilant Orange Creams

Orange creams make a great fresh and healthy snack. The milk and vanilla combined with tangy orange juice creates a delicious drink that is enjoyable for both kids and adults alike. The frozen concentrate also makes it a powerful ally in fighting the torrid heat of summer,

6 ounces frozen orange juice
    concentrate
1 cup low-fat milk
1 cup cold water

1/3 cup granulated sugar
1 teaspoon vanilla extract

Put all ingredients into a blender and mix thoroughly. Pour into a glass and serve with a straw. *Makes 4 6-ounce servings.*

Strawberry Daiquiri

The strawberry daiquiri's sheer simplicity, combined with icy refreshing flavors, makes it a natural Florida cocktail. Rum is plentiful, and Florida strawberries are perfect for these juice-filled daiquiris. Like Florida oranges, Florida strawberries are juicy and their flavor is the best!

1 pint fresh strawberries
Juice of 1/2 medium orange
1 tablespoon powdered sugar

6 ounces light rum
Crushed ice

Wash the strawberries gently under cool water and cut off the stems. Place all ingredients in blender. Blend for 60 seconds on high speed until smooth. Serve in a daiquiri glass with a straw and paper umbrella, and enjoy! Feel free to experiment with other fruits such as bananas or watermelon for exciting variations. *Makes 3–4 servings.*

Perfect Planter's Punch

Wildly popular in the 1970s, planter's punch was the drink of tropical paradises and wispy dreams. Florida has contributed its fine cane sugar and zesty lemons to this tasty and power-packed drink in which the sweetness of the rum and sugar blend subtly with the bitters and the sourness of the lemon. A comeback in the popularity of planter's punch seems inevitable.

6 ounces fresh lime juice (approximately 1/2 medium lime)
3/4 cup powdered sugar

2 cups plus 2 ounces light rum
3 cups crushed ice
12 dashes Angostura bitters

In a cocktail shaker stir the lime juice and sugar until the sugar is completely dissolved. Add the rum, ice, and bitters and shake well. Pour into a collins glass unstrained. *Makes 6 servings.*

Mojo Mojito

This classic Latin cocktail is experiencing vibrant popularity in restaurants and bars throughout southern and central Florida. It has even been ordered in a recent James Bond Movie. The mojo mojito, with its sweet minty zing, brings an exotic flair to any party, and conjures up images of steamy Florida or Havana nights.

3 sprigs of fresh mint
2 teaspoons powdered sugar
3 tablespoons lemon juice (lime juice may be substituted)
1 1/2 ounces light rum

Crushed ice
1 ounce club soda
Lemon wedge (a lime wedge may be substituted)
Sugar cane stick to garnish (if available)

In a tall thin glass crush 2 sprigs of mint against the glass. Add the sugar and lemon juice and mix thoroughly. Add rum and ice and mix well. Top with a shot of club soda, the remaining mint sprig, and a lemon wedge. Stir and garnish with sugar cane. *Makes 1 serving.*

Cuba Libre

Our favorite way to drink rum and coke is with a lime. The sour tang of the lime creates an exotic fusion with the sweetness of the cola and the richness of the dark rum. In the Caribbean and other parts of Latin America, this classic concoction is called a Cuba libre. One sip in the sultry tropical air and you will want to shout out loud through the salsa music, "Free Cuba!"

1 1/2 ounces dark rum
3 ounces Coca-Cola®
Crushed ice
Lime wedge

In an old fashioned glass, pour dark rum and Coca-Cola® over crushed ice. Stir and garnish with a lime wedge. *Makes 1 serving.*

❧

Spring Hill Bloody Mary

The bloody Mary can be as individual and unique as the person mak-
ing it. Whether using clam juice or beef stock, V8 juice®, celery, or
onions, no two recipes are ever identical. This recipe has been tested
many times throughout the years, and the results are a true winner. It
is the slight hint of clams mixed with low-pulp tomato that blends eas-
ily with vegetable salts and the cleanliness of the vodka. Enjoy it as a
daytime treat or an evening cocktail with friends.

32 ounces Clamato® juice
   (tomato juice may be sub-
   stituted)
12 ounces vodka
1/4 teaspoon garlic salt
1/4 teaspoon onion salt
1/3 teaspoon celery salt
2 teaspoons chili powder

10 dashes Tabasco Sauce®
   (other hot pepper sauces
   may be substituted)
5 dashes Worcestershire sauce
3 Spanish pimiento-stuffed
   olives
Celery stalks
1 lemon, cut into wedges

Mix all ingredients together in a large airtight container and
shake very well. Let stand at least 15 minutes in the refrigerator to allow all the flavors to mix together. In a tall glass, pour
the bloody Mary over ice and serve with a celery stalk and
lemon wedge. *Makes 6 8-ounce servings.*

Piña Colada

The sweetest, creamiest and richest of all the tropical drinks, piña colada was invented in Puerto Rico, and then spread throughout the Caribbean to Florida. It is rumored to have been Ernest Hemingway's favorite cocktail when he was in Key West. If you cannot make it to Key West to enjoy a piña colada, any beach (or your backyard, with a bucket of sand to put you in the mood) will make an equally legitimate setting.

8 ounces Jamaican rum
8 ounces coconut cream
12 ounces pineapple juice
4 ounces orange juice

1 cup crushed ice
4 pineapple wedges
4 maraschino cherries

Combine rum, coconut cream, pineapple juice, and orange juice in a cocktail shaker. Shake vigorously. In a highball glass filled with ice, pour in the rum mixture and garnish with pineapple wedge and cherry. For a frozen cocktail, blend the first 4 ingredients with crushed ice. Pour into a daiquiri glass and garnish with pineapple wedge and cherry. *Makes 4 10-ounce servings.*

Beach Margarita

The world over, margaritas conjure up thoughts of Florida beaches and the "good life," as described by our unofficial state songwriter, Jimmy Buffet. For those who live in Florida, the search for truly outstanding margaritas has created many memories that are sure to conjure up a smile. Why not? It's not easy to find the perfect mix of sour, sweetness, salt, and the succulent flavors of tequila.

1 1/2 ounces gold tequila
1/2 ounce triple sec or
   Cointreau®
Juice of 1 medium lime

1/4 cup crushed ice
1 lime, cut into wedges
Margarita salt (available at
   liquor stores)

Mix tequila, triple sec, and lime juice with crushed ice in a cocktail shaker. Rub the rim of a margarita glass with a lime wedge. Dip the glass into the salt, coating the entire rim. Strain tequila mixture into the glass, with or without ice, and serve with a lime wedge. For a frozen margarita, blend ingredients for 30 seconds with crushed ice, and pour into salt-rimmed glass. *Makes 1 serving.*

Appetizers

Tangy Florida Seafood Dip

This scrumptious dip was originally made with minced clams and was always a party favorite. It had a rich and creamy taste and was easy to prepare. It has since been adapted to fit the Florida bounty, substituting bay scallops and shrimp for the clams, and adding lemon juice and pepper sauce. The new version is even more luscious, and the lemon's sourness matches sublimely with sweeter seafood. It has quickly gone from a party hit to a legend.

2 medium loaves round sourdough bread
1 teaspoon extra virgin olive oil
1 clove garlic, minced
1/4 pound bay scallops
1/4 pound medium shrimp, peeled and deveined
8 ounces regular cream cheese, softened
8 ounces light cream cheese, softened
1/4 cup fresh squeezed lemon juice

2 tablespoons fresh Italian parsley, chopped
2 teaspoons fresh basil, chopped
1 1/2 teaspoons Worcestershire sauce
1 teaspoon Tabasco Sauce®
1/4 cup scallions, minced
1/2 teaspoon salt
1/2 teaspoon fresh ground black pepper

Cut a 5-inch diameter hole in the top of one of the loaves of sourdough bread. Scoop out the insides and set aside.

Heat olive oil in small frying pan on medium-low. Sauté garlic for 1 minute, and then add scallops and shrimp. Cook gently over medium heat until opaque, approximately 3 minutes. Remove from heat. Mix remaining ingredients in bowl, blending well. Chop scallops and shrimp into small pieces, and add to cream cheese mixture. Spoon the mixture into the bread bowl, top with bread "lid," and wrap completely in foil. Cook in 250°F oven for 2 hours until soft and warm.

Cut the second loaf into 1-inch pieces. Serve the dip with sourdough pieces and insides of first loaf. *Makes 8 appetizer-size portions.*

Original Heart of Palm Dip

A staple dish dating back to undergraduate years spent at Florida State University. The Heart of Palm Dip was inspired by a baked artichoke dip. The final result, however, would not at all resemble the original. Years of experimentation with the ingredients eventually yielded the most famous, successful, and original dish in this cookbook.

This dip was born to be social, as it was first prepared for a party as guests were arriving. As the crowd entered, few made it past the kitchen without stopping to explore the origin of the wonderful smells wafting through the air. Once served, it took some time for the guests to try it. Fresh food was not yet the norm for this college crowd, and new adventures in culinary delights take a little time to develop momentum. Once they tried the dip, however, the crowd was won over.

It has since been made many times and requested by many people. The most important tip for this recipe is to use a high quality parmesan cheese. Make it for any event: summer, winter, casual, or formal. If you have pride in creating it, your friends' salutations and smiles will be your just reward.

1 tablespoon extra virgin olive oil

2 large garlic cloves, finely chopped

2 14-ounce cans heart of palm, finely chopped (reserve the liquid from one can)

1/4 cup dry white wine (equal amount of pilsner-style beer can be substituted)

1/3 cup fine Italian-style dry bread crumbs

1/4 cup parmesan cheese, finely grated

1/2 teaspoon salt

1/2 teaspoon freshly ground black pepper

Heat the olive oil in a heavy saucepan. Add the garlic and sauté slowly until garlic turns a golden brown. Slowly add in heart of palm, stirring constantly. Add the wine or beer and gently stir for 10 minutes in order to steam out the alcohol. Lower the heat and slowly begin adding the bread crumbs, constantly stirring. If the mixture becomes too dry, add a small amount of reserved heart of palm liquid. Continue cooking over low heat for approximately 15 minutes. Fold in the cheese, salt, and pepper, stirring an additional 5 minutes.

This dish is perfect for just about any event. It can be a centerpiece of a cocktail party, a side dish, or even a tailgate dip. Serve with butter crackers or toasted bread and enjoy. *Makes 8 appetizer-size portions.*

Heart of Palm Cocktail

This simple but unique dish is a perfect addition to cocktail parties, picnics, or dinners. It can also be served as a side dish, or perhaps on a bed of lettuce as a main course salad. The olives and feta compliment the tart brininess of the heart of palm, and the olive oil gives the dish a nice balance. Try experimenting with other crumbled cheeses, such as Gorgonzola or Roquefort.

2 14-ounce cans heart of
   palm, drained
1 14-ounce can pitted black
   olives, drained
1/3 cup crumbled feta cheese
   (crumbled goat cheese may
   be substituted)
2 tablespoons extra virgin
   olive oil

1 tablespoon fresh basil, finely
   chopped (fresh oregano
   may be substituted)
1/4 teaspoon salt
1/4 teaspoon fresh ground
   black pepper

Cut heart of palm stalks into quarter-inch-thick coins; cut black olives in half. Combine all ingredients and gently toss, coating with the olive oil. Refrigerate 1 to 2 hours. Serve in a glass bowl with toast points. *Makes 6 appetizer-size portions.*

❦

Mussels with Citrus Beurre Blanc

A dish at one of our favorite Tampa waterside restaurants inspired this recipe. We have jazzed up the original to make our own French Florida creation. The secret is that mussels with citrus beurre blanc are quick yet elegant, a dish that can be served as an entrée, appetizer, or snack. Accompanied by good French bread, this dish will satisfy the most distinguished of palates.

1 teaspoon extra virgin olive
    oil
1/4 cup salted butter
2 large cloves garlic, finely
    chopped
1 medium shallot, finely
    chopped
36 black mussels (rinsed in
    fresh water with beards
    removed)
3/4 cup dry white wine
1 teaspoon fresh basil, finely
    chopped

1 teaspoon fresh cilantro,
    chopped
1 tablespoon fresh chives,
    chopped
1 teaspoon roux (see below)
Juice of 1 medium orange
Juice of 1 medium lemon
1/2 cup half-and-half
Salt and fresh ground black
    pepper to taste

Roux
2 tablespoons salted butter
2 tablespoons all-purpose flour

Melt the butter over low heat. Stir in flour and cook over low heat for 2 minutes until a paste is formed. Remove the roux from heat and set aside.

Make roux and set aside.

    Heat olive oil and butter together in large pot over medium heat, then add garlic and shallots. Cook until shallots become transparent, approximately 3–4 minutes. Add mussels and cook until the shells open. Add the wine and herbs and cook for approximately 1 minute to cook off the alcohol. Using a slotted spoon or tongs, move mussels to a platter. Whisk the roux into the pot. Add orange juice and half the lemon juice. Then, slowly whisk in the half-and-half and bring to a simmer. Once sauce begins to thicken, add mussels back to the pan, stirring them gently into the sauce. Heat for 2 minutes and sprinkle with fresh herbs. Season with salt and fresh ground black pepper to taste.

Pour entire contents of the pot into a large, shallow bowl and serve with toasted French bread. Champagne or a dry white wine, such as Sauvignon Blanc, makes a nice accompaniment. *Makes 4 appetizer-size portions or 2 entrée-size portions.*

Oysters on the Half Shell

Florida oysters are smaller than the popular Pacific Northwest oysters. However, their flavor makes up for their size: the rich, smooth flavor makes them a delicacy for all who are lucky enough to indulge. During heavy rains, you can taste the fresh water from the bountiful Apalachicola River; when the river is low the oysters become a bit saltier. Truly a Florida must-have!

Some consider raw oysters a delicacy while others find them repulsive. To the latter we send our condolences. For those of you afraid of being ill, read the literature, understand your own health, and be careful. Any month that contains the letter R (September–April) is the proper eating time, or so the old story goes in Florida. These are the cold months, during which it is safe to eat oysters because the bacteria that causes food poisoning is less likely to be present. If you can find them pasteurized, you can eat them any time!

4 dozen fresh oysters
2 lemons, cut into wedges
1/2 cup horseradish
1/2 cup cocktail sauce

Your favorite brand of hot
pepper sauce
4 dozen saltine crackers

When oysters are well iced, they will last approximately 3 days. Shuck the oysters (pry them open with an oyster shucker or dull thick-bladed knife) and either slurp 'em down plain or experiment with variations of hot sauce, lemon, horseradish, cocktail sauce, and saltine crackers. Beer is a good match, but a big California Chardonnay will also make a wonderful partner. *Serves 4.*

Big Money Oysters Rockefeller

Oysters Rockefeller is a classic American hors d'oeuvre, served wherever oysters are abundant. In Florida, the Apalachicola Bay produces some of the country's finest types. The dish is somewhat seasonal, in that the oysters are best during the cooler months and the richness of the sauce is not well suited for the high heat of Florida summers. Regardless of when you have Oysters Rockefeller, you will enjoy the dish for its timeless quality and elegance.

For ease of preparation, the dish is broken into four major steps. Your time and effort will be rewarded as your guests swoon at the first luscious bite.

Step 1: Make the béchamel

1 cup whole milk	*1 bay leaf*
1 medium shallot, peeled and	*1 medium carrot, quartered*
chopped	*1 sprig Italian parsley*
5 large cloves garlic, whole	
1/2 teaspoon crushed black	
pepper	

Add all ingredients to milk in medium saucepan. Leave on low heat for 10–15 minutes, being careful not to boil or scald the milk. Remove from the heat and set aside to cool. Strain and discard the herbs and vegetables.

Step 2: Make the roux
2 tablespoons salted butter
2 tablespoons flour

Melt butter over low heat in a small saucepan. Stir in flour and cook over low heat for 2 minutes until a paste is formed. (This is the roux.) Remove from heat.

Step 3: Make the Mornay sauce
Roux (see above)
Béchamel sauce (see above)
1/2 cup fresh grated Parmigiano-Reggiano cheese
2 tablespoons heavy cream

In the same saucepan, return the roux to a low heat, whisking in 1/4 cup of the béchamel sauce until incorporated. Slowly whisk in the rest of the béchamel sauce until incorporated. Stir in the Parmigiano-Reggiano and cream over low heat until the sauce thickens.

Step 4: Finish the dish

1/4 pound spinach, finely chopped
3 strips bacon, cooked until crisp and crumbled
1 tablespoon orange juice
1 tablespoon dry sherry

Salt and fresh ground black pepper to taste
2 dozen fresh shucked oysters (keeping the deeper half shell)

Mix finely chopped spinach and crumbled bacon into the Mornay sauce. Add the orange juice and sherry. Cook for 5 minutes or until sauce thickens, adding salt and pepper to taste. Lay oysters in the shell on a large baking sheet, keeping one inch between each shell. Spoon 1 tablespoon of sauce onto each oyster. Cook at 350°F for 15 minutes. Remove and let stand for 5 minutes. Serve warm. *Makes 6 servings of 4 oysters each.*

Crabby Stuffed Mushrooms

Everyone has their version of stuffed mushrooms—they are, in fact, one of the more common restaurant appetizers found in Florida, and why not? Stuffed mushrooms are simple to make, go with most foods, and can be served during any season.

2 dozen fresh large white
    mushrooms
1 tablespoon extra virgin olive
    oil
2 large cloves garlic
1/2 medium Spanish onion,
    diced
1 tablespoon fresh basil, finely
    chopped
1 tablespoon fresh parsley,
    finely chopped
1/4 dry white wine
1/2 cup bread crumbs
1 tablespoon pecans, chopped

1 teaspoon fresh thyme, finely
    chopped
1 teaspoon hot pepper sauce of
    your choice
1/2 cup seafood stock (chicken
    stock may be substituted)
1/4 pound lump or claw crab
    meat
1/2 teaspoon salt
1/2 teaspoon fresh ground
    black pepper
freshly grated parmesan
    cheese (optional)

Rinse, skin,* and de-stem mushrooms. Cut stems and outer skin into a fine dice or rough paste.

In a large sauce pan, add olive oil and sauté the garlic and onions until they become translucent. Add diced mushrooms, basil and parsley, cooking approximately 4 minutes (water from mushrooms will begin to steam out). Add wine and continue to cook for 3 minutes in order to steam out the alcohol. Add bread crumbs, chopped pecans, thyme, and hot pepper sauce. Slowly begin stirring in the stock, until it forms a moist ball. Fold in the crab meat, being careful not to break it up. Add salt and pepper. Fill each mushroom cap with the crab stuffing.

Place stuffed mushrooms on a cookie sheet or baking pan and bake at 350°F for 30 minutes. Near the end of the baking process, the mushrooms can be sprinkled with freshly grated parmesan cheese if desired. Serve on a colorful platter for added flair. *Makes 6 appetizer-size portions.*

* To skin mushrooms, peel back the fine layer of skin from the underside of the cap to the top of the mushroom.

Gulf Coast Ceviche

Our first true ceviche experience was in San Jose, Costa Rica, at a little Masqueria, or seafood restaurant, near the University of Costa Rica. The flavors were striking and showcased the seafood of Central America. We have highlighted the Florida bounty by adapting the recipe to local flavors and ingredients with delicious results. You can serve it in a traditional style with a spoon, or perhaps try it with tortilla chips or hard crusty bread as a new American classic.

1/3 pound fresh sea scallops
1/3 pound fresh medium shrimp, peeled and deveined
1/3 pound fresh grouper (use flounder if grouper is not available)
1/4 cup fresh cilantro, chopped
2 large cloves garlic, finely minced
1 medium fresh habanero pepper, seeded and finely chopped
Juice of 2 large limes

2 tablespoons gold tequila
2 tablespoons plus 1 teaspoon extra virgin olive oil
1/2 medium green bell pepper, seeded and diced
1/2 medium red or yellow bell pepper, seeded and diced
2 large oranges, skinned, seeded, and cubed
Salt and fresh ground black pepper to taste
1 medium mango, cubed
1 small Spanish onion, diced

Step 1: Seafood Preparation
Chop scallops, shrimp, and grouper into quarter-inch cubes and place in bowl with 1/8 cup cilantro, 1 clove of garlic, and 1/8 teaspoon chopped habanero pepper. Squeeze in juice of half a lime and add the tequila. Let stand in refrigerator for at least 2 hours to overnight. If the seafood marinates longer than 12 hours, cooking is not required.

Heat one teaspoon of oil in a sauté pan, then add the seafood and entire marinade. Cook approximately 2 minutes. Remove to a fresh bowl and let cool. You do not need to cook the seafood completely, as the marinade will finish the cooking process.

Step 2: Salsa Preparation
Combine remaining garlic and habanero pepper with the bell peppers, oranges, mango, and onion in a large bowl. Add 1/8 cup cilantro to the bowl and toss lightly. Add the seafood, juice of 1 lime, and 2 teaspoons of olive oil, again tossing lightly. Add salt and freshly ground black pepper to taste, and let stand for at least 30 minutes. The other half lime should be cut into wedges for a garnish.

Serve with tortilla chips, crusty bread, or a big spoon. *Makes 6 appetizer-size portions.*

Gulf coast ceviche can also be used as a complement for tropical fish, pork, or chicken dishes.

Florida Citrus Salsa

Salsa is a great staple for social gatherings in Florida. Why not make your own and create a party showcase? By using a varied selection of fresh fruits, peppers, tomatoes, and herbs, salsa can accompany almost any occasion. We are firm believers of the spicy food proverb "The warmer the weather, the hotter the flavor!"

1 large clove garlic, chopped	*1 large tangerine*
1/2 medium green bell pepper, diced	*1/4 small grapefruit*
	1 large orange
1/2 medium red or yellow bell pepper, diced	*Juice of 1 1/2 medium limes*
	2 teaspoons extra virgin olive oil
1 fresh habanero pepper, chopped	*Salt and freshly ground black pepper to taste*
1 small red onion, diced	
1/4 cup fresh cilantro, chopped	*Lime wedges for garnish*

Combine garlic, bell and habanero peppers, onion, and cilantro in a large bowl. Peel the tangerine, grapefruit, and orange with a knife and cut into small cubes, being careful to remove the seeds and center pith. Add the fruit, lime juice, and olive oil; lightly toss. Add salt and pepper to taste and chill for at least thirty minutes. Garnish with lime wedges and a sprig of cilantro.

Serve with tortilla chips, corn chips, or plantain chips, or try using as a condiment for tropical fish, pork, or chicken main courses. *Makes 2 cups of salsa.*

Salads

Tarpon Springs Greek Salad

*Almost everyone loves a traditional Greek salad. However, in Florida
we have a unique twist. Tarpon Springs is a small Greek community
north of St. Petersburg that is dominated by sponge docks and excellent
Greek cuisine. The Greek salads in Tarpon Springs always have a hid-
den scoop of potato salad in the middle. This variation is present
throughout central Florida and makes an interesting variation to a
classic dish.*

Greek Salad

*1/2 medium head iceberg let-
    tuce
1/2 medium head romaine let-
    tuce
1 cup Greek-style potato salad
    (see below)
1 small red onion, cut into
    rings
1 large Ruskin tomato, cut
    into wedges*

*1 medium cucumber, sliced
16 Kalamata olives
8 medium pepperoncini
1/3 cup feta cheese
6 anchovy fillets (these may be
    omitted if preferred)
Greek-style vinaigrette dress-
    ing (see below)*

In a large salad bowl or lipped plate layer the lettuces, alter-
nating the iceberg and Romaine, around the center. Place the
potato salad in the center of the lettuce and cover with the red
onion, followed by the tomato and cucumber. Add the olives
and pepperoncini and sprinkle with feta cheese. Top with
anchovy fillets if desired. Serve with a Greek-style vinaigrette
dressing. *Yields 6 salad portions.*

Greek-style Potato Salad
Boil potatoes until almost tender. Remove from water, let cool,

*6 medium Yukon gold potatoes
1 medium white onion, finely
    chopped
1/4 cup extra virgin olive oil
1 tablespoon mayonnaise*

*Juice of 1/2 large lemon
Salt and fresh ground black
    pepper to taste
1 teaspoon fresh oregano,
    finely chopped*

then peel. Cut into half- to 1-inch pieces and combine with onion, olive oil, mayonnaise, and lemon juice in a large bowl; add salt and pepper to taste. Sprinkle with oregano and toss lightly. Chill for 1 hour.

Greek-style Vinaigrette Dressing
Whisk all ingredients together. Set aside until ready to use.

1 cup extra virgin olive oil　　　*1/4 teaspoon salt*
1/4 cup white wine vinegar　　　*1/4 teaspoon fresh ground*
1 tablespoon dried oregano　　　　*black pepper*

Chilly Dilly Shrimps
a.k.a. "Shrimps à la Sergio"

Once, after preparing a dinner party, we had a few leftover shrimp. Scampi is passé and cocktail trivial, so what to do? Yogurt became the focus ingredient, and the dish came out fresh and cool. When we served it to our friend Sergio he claimed it was the best shrimp dish he had ever tried. It has been a standing order ever since. For Sergio's acceptance and everyone else's enjoyment, we have included it here for you to try.

1 pound fresh large Gulf
    shrimp, peeled and
    deveined
2 large cloves garlic, minced
2 medium lemons
2 tablespoons fresh dill,
    chopped

3/4 cup plain low-fat yogurt
1 tablespoon mayonnaise
1/2 teaspoon salt
1/2 teaspoon freshly ground
    black pepper

Marinate the shrimp in the garlic, juice of 1 lemon, and 1 teaspoon of fresh dill for 1 hour. Steam shrimp for 4–5 minutes; they should still be slightly translucent. Remove and set aside. The shrimp will continue to cook through lingering heat, and will come out perfectly tender once they have cooled.

In a separate bowl, combine yogurt, mayonnaise, and the remaining lemon juice and dill. Add in the cooled shrimp, as well as the salt and fresh ground black pepper. Chill for at least 30 minutes. Serve in a glass bowl with toothpicks and a garnish of dill. *Makes 6 to 8 appetizer-size portions.*

☙

Papaya, Tomato, and Cilantro Salad

For many people, papaya is not an easily acquired taste or smell. However, once given a fair chance, papayas offer near endless options for fruit accompaniments. This salad recipe makes a great introduction to this exotic tropical fruit. As the flavors of the cilantro and tomato blend with the papaya, they create a delicious infusion of colors, flavors, and textures.

One medium, firm papaya
4 medium plum tomatoes
1/3 cup fresh cilantro, finely chopped
1/8 cup extra virgin olive oil

Seed both the papaya and the tomatoes and cut into small quarter-inch cubes. Finely chop the cilantro and toss together with the fruits. Refrigerate for 30 minutes before serving. Drizzle with olive oil, lightly toss and serve. *Yields 6 salad portions.*

Classic Caesar Salad

The origin of the Caesar Salad is often debated. The most common claims place its origins in Mexico or southern California. While the claim cannot be settled here, we would like to thank the inventor for providing Florida seafood fans a perfect accompaniment to their meals! The crisp, fresh flavors of this dressing go wonderfully with a main course with crab, lobster, shrimp, or almost any Florida fish. Once you have made it yourself, the "bottled stuff" will never taste the same.

1 head Romaine lettuce, washed and torn into bite-size pieces
3 cups homemade croutons (see below)

1 cup Caesar dressing (see below)
1/2 cup fresh grated parmesan
4–5 anchovy fillets (optional)

Toss lettuce, croutons, and dressing well in large bowl. Sprinkle parmesan over the salad and toss lightly. Place anchovy fillets on top if desired. *Yields 8 salad or 4 main course portions.*

Croutons

1 small, stale loaf French or Italian bread, cubed
3 tablespoons extra virgin olive oil
1 large clove garlic, minced

1 teaspoon dried basil
1 teaspoon dried oregano
1/4 teaspoon salt
1/4 teaspoon pepper

Toss all ingredients in a large bowl, making sure to coat the bread with oil, garlic, and seasonings. Broil for approximately 5 minutes in baking dish, tossing once, until golden brown. Set aside.

Caesar Dressing

1 large pasteurized egg yolk
2 medium garlic cloves,
minced
2 small anchovy fillets,
chopped (1/2 teaspoon
anchovy paste may be
substituted)
1 teaspoon Dijon mustard
1 teaspoon white wine vinegar

1 teaspoon fresh ground black
pepper
1/2 teaspoon salt
1/2 teaspoon Worcestershire
sauce
1/3 cup extra virgin olive oil
Juice of 1 large lemon
3 dashes hot pepper sauce of
your choice

Whisk all ingredients together by hand or put in a food processor until emulsified. The dressing can be served immediately or, for best results, let stand in the refrigerator 30 minutes. Store covered in the refrigerator for up to 2 days. *Makes approximately 1 cup of salad dressing.*

Note: Because there is raw egg yolk in the dressing, use fresh, cold eggs and do not keep for more than 48 hours.

Florida Lobster and Blue Crab Salad in Avocado

A seafood avocado salad is a delectable dish perfect for a lunch center-piece or a dinner appetizer. The rich creaminess of the avocado blends with the crab and lobster meat and the cilantro gives it a touch of the exotic and draws all of the flavors together. You can try adding a few of your favorite flavors as well to personalize this wonderful creation.

1 tablespoon salted butter
1 large clove garlic, finely chopped
1/2 pound Florida spiny lobster tail, removed from shell
1 tablespoon fresh cilantro, finely chopped
2 scallions, finely chopped
1 large plum tomato, seeded and chopped
1 tablespoon plain low-fat yogurt

1 1/2 teaspoons mayonnaise
4 tablespoons fresh squeezed orange juice
1/2 pound blue crab meat, cooked and cleaned (stone crab may be substituted)
Salt and fresh ground black pepper to taste
2 small ripe Florida avocados*, halved and pitted
Juice of 1/2 medium lime
Lime wedges
1 dash Tabasco Sauce®

Heat butter in heavy skillet on a medium-high heat. Add garlic and sauté for 3 minutes. Add lobster to the skillet and sauté for an additional 3 minutes. Remove from heat and chop lobster into small cubes.

Combine cilantro, scallions, and tomato together with yogurt and mayonnaise. Add orange and lime juices, plus a dash of Tabasco Sauce®, and toss. Gently mix in cooled lobster and crab meat. Add salt and pepper to taste. Place mixture in the center of halved avocados and squeeze lime wedge over the top. Refrigerate for at least 1 hour. Serve with white wine or a tropical beer such as Kalik, Red Stripe, Ybor Gold, or Hurricane Reef. *Yields 4 salad servings.*

*Avocados are best when ripened to the point that the tip of the fruit yields under pressure of the thumb.

∞

Soups

Blue Crab Bisque

Not to be taken lightly, this bisque is the queen of Florida soups. We first enjoyed blue crab bisque in Cedar Key, and since have pursued a quest for the perfect bisque. If made with love, this recipe should come very close. Enjoy it on your own special day, even if it is to celebrate a Tuesday sunset, a Sunday at the beach, or just because you are feeling inspired. The best time to enjoy good food such as this is when you have the time to make it yourself and the time to enjoy it.

1/8 cup finely chopped celery	2 cups low-fat milk
1/4 cup finely chopped onion	1 pound blue crab meat, cleaned
1/4 cup salted butter	1/2 teaspoon salt
1/4 cup all purpose flour	1/4 teaspoon ground white pepper
2 cups half-and-half	1/4 teaspoon ground red pepper

In the top of a double boiler, cook the celery and onion together in melted butter until soft. Stir in the flour until well mixed. Slowly pour in the half-and-half, followed by the milk, stirring slowly and constantly. Continue to cook over boiling water, stirring occasionally, until thickened. Add the crab and continue cooking until thicker. Do not over-stir at this point or the crab meat will break up. Add the salt and white and red peppers, adjusting for taste.

Remember that this bisque should not be hurried. The longer it takes to make, the more heavenly it will become. *Yields 4 servings.*

✑

Tampa Garbanzo Bean Soup

This is a delicious and hearty soup that will work for all seasons. The sights, smells, and tastes of Tampa's historic Ybor City inspired this rendition of a classic Cuban-style soup. It is one of the more common soups to be found in Tampa, and with some argument, the best. This particular recipe was inspired by a bowl of soup enjoyed in Ybor City many years ago. Garbanzo bean soup can usually be found in two different styles, one more brothy and one a bit more creamy and starchy. Presented here is the style with a greater emphasis on broth.

1 large Spanish onion, chopped
4 large cloves garlic, minced
1 tablespoon extra virgin olive oil
1/2 pound Spanish chorizo sausage
1 teaspoon dried basil
1 teaspoon dried oregano
1 bay leaf
1 small red chili pepper, seeded and finely minced

1 tablespoon saffron
1/4 cup pimento-stuffed green olives
1 15-ounce can chickpeas, drained*
4 cups chicken stock
4 cups water
1/2 teaspoon cumin
Salt and fresh ground black pepper to taste

Using a large, heavy stockpot or slow cooker, sauté the onions and garlic in the olive oil until tender. Add the sausage, dried herbs, bay leaf, red chili pepper, and saffron and continue to sauté for approximately 6 minutes. Add the olives and cook 5 additional minutes at low heat. Mix in the chickpeas and continue to cook for another 5 minutes. Pour in the chicken stock and water and bring to a simmer. Stir in the cumin and then cook over a low heat for at least 4 hours. Taste every hour to gauge if additional spices are needed. Add salt and pepper to taste. Serve with Cuban bread for a hearty meal. *Makes 8 cups of soup.*

*If using dried beans, soak overnight in a large pot of water in the refrigerator with 1 teaspoon of salt.

Oyster Stew

Oyster Stew is just the thing during the cool winter months to warm your bones and increase your vigor. It can be prepared year-round, however, as pasteurized oysters may be used in place of fresh—and soup is great after a rainy day in the summer. This recipe is also a good way to introduce someone to oysters if they are not bold enough to eat them raw.

1/4 medium white onion, diced	1/4 cup dry white wine
2 tablespoons butter	3 cups low-fat milk
1 dozen cleaned oysters (reserve juice)	2 tablespoons all purpose flour
1 teaspoon fresh thyme, finely chopped	1/2 teaspoon white pepper

In a large medium soup pot, sauté the onion in a tablespoon of butter until it becomes translucent (but do not caramelize the onion). Add the oysters and thyme and sauté for about 3 minutes, and then add the wine and steam out the alcohol for 2 minutes. Reduce the heat to low and slowly add in 2 1/2 cups of the milk, stirring constantly. Cook at a simmer for approximately 30 minutes. Meanwhile, combine flour and remaining 1/2 cup milk. After 30 minutes, add the milk and flour mixture to the soup pot. Simmer for an additional 30 minutes. Finish by stirring in the white pepper and remaining tablespoon of butter. Serve in deep soup bowls with plenty of saltine crackers. *Makes 4 cups of soup.*

∽

Gator Black Bean Chili

While alligators are now abundant, this was not always the case. Alligators were nearly wiped out early in the twentieth century, but they have made a remarkable comeback. Today, there are nearly two million of the big reptiles lurking in Florida swamps, rivers, canals, lakes, and sometimes even swimming pools. They are hunted with strict limits, but their recent proliferation might indicate that an increase in tag limits is needed. Look for the meat in specialty grocery stores, fish markets, and online purveyors. It's great when prepared correctly, as in this chili.

2 tablespoons extra virgin
  olive oil
2 large cloves garlic, minced
1 large yellow onion, chopped
1 small green bell pepper,
  chopped
3 small red chili peppers*
1/2 pound fresh alligator
  meat, cut into half-inch
  cubes
2 teaspoons fresh oregano,
  finely chopped

2 tablespoons fresh basil,
  chopped
3 14.5-ounce cans stewed
  tomatoes
1 15-ounce can of black beans,
  drained**
2 tablespoons chili powder
1 teaspoon salt
1/2 teaspoon fresh ground
  black pepper

Heat olive oil over medium heat. Sauté the garlic, onion, bell pepper, and chili peppers for 5 minutes until the onions become translucent. Once the onions begin to caramelize, add the gator meat, dried herbs, and chili powder. Sauté until the meat is completely cooked. Meanwhile, puree 1 can of tomatoes and add to the pot. Pour in the other 2 cans of stewed tomatoes "as is." Add the black beans, salt, and black pepper and cook over low to medium heat for at least 4 hours. Serve with shredded or cubed cheddar or colby cheese and a loaf of good rye bread. *Makes 6 cups of soup.*

*A habanero pepper may be substituted for the chilies if you want a fiery hot chili.

**If using dried beans, soak overnight in a large pot of water in the refrigerator with 1 teaspoon of salt.

Vidalia (French-style) Onion Soup

This is a Southern version of traditional French-style onion soup. While the onions are typically from Georgia, it would be unfair to mention Florida cuisine without properly acknowledging some of the wonderful products our neighboring states contribute to our bounty. This soup works itself perfectly into Florida cool-weather cuisine, and it's easy enough to make that you can always have a pot ready.

1 large Vidalia onion (a red or sweet Spanish onion may be substituted), cut into thin rings
1 small clove garlic
2 tablespoons salted butter, divided
1 tablespoon all-purpose flour
1 cup dry white wine
2 cups chicken stock (for a vegetarian option, substitute equal parts vegetable stock)
2 thick slices toasted French bread
2 slices mozzarella cheese
Salt and fresh ground black pepper to taste

Sauté the onions and garlic in 1 tablespoon of butter until onions become clear but not caramelized. Add the other tablespoon of butter and the flour, stirring for 3–4 minutes until a roux is formed. Add the wine and cook for 2 minutes to steam out the alcohol. Add the stock, 1 cup at a time, about every 5 minutes. Simmer the soup approximately 1 hour until it begins to thicken slightly. Add salt and black pepper to taste.

Place toast at the bottom of a large oven-safe soup bowl. Cover with soup and top with a slice of mozzarella cheese. Place under the broiler for approximately 2 minutes until cheese begins to brown. Place the hot bowl on a plate to serve. *Makes 2 hearty servings.*

༺ல

Sandwiches

Spicy Shrimp Po' Boy

The New Orleans style Po' Boy is the South's entry into the great American sandwich battle. Hero, hoagie, grinder, sub, and po' boy—all are wonderful variations of a hearty meal wrapped in fresh bread. It is the bounty of the Gulf of Mexico that makes for such a natural connection between Floridian and Cajun cuisine, with the primary differences being that in Florida there is a little less butter and a bit more citrus.

1 pound large fresh shrimp, peeled and deveined
1/2 large lemon
2 tablespoons Cajun seasoning
2 tablespoons all-purpose flour
1/4 cup seafood or chicken stock

2 tablespoon salted butter
1 large clove garlic
1 tablespoon Tabasco Sauce®
1/4 cup dry white wine
1 loaf French bread or 2 French baguettes, cut for four sandwiches

Step 1: Prepare the Shrimp
Marinate shrimp in the juice from a quarter of a lemon and 1 tablespoon Cajun seasoning.

Step 2: Liquid roux
Mix the flour, remaining Cajun seasoning, and stock together in a separate bowl until smooth.

Step 3: Sandwich Filling
In a hot sauté pan, melt the butter and add finely chopped garlic; sauté until translucent. Add shrimp and Tabasco Sauce®, sautéing each side of the shrimp approximately 1 minute. Pour in the wine, and then add the liquid roux. Cook an additional 4 minutes, stirring and flipping the shrimp to keep them from burning or sticking.

Butter each side of a sliced French baguette. Spoon the shrimp onto it and press into a pan under a heavy warm iron skillet, with foil on the top of the bread, for about 3 minutes. Serve warm. *Makes 4 sandwiches.*

⌦

Soft-shell Crab Po' Boy

Blue crabs molt their shells in order to grow larger. After dropping their old shell, the new shell remains very soft for a brief period; this is when the crabs are most vulnerable. At this time, the prized crabs have their richest and sweetest taste, and are entirely edible (soft shell and all). One common way of enjoying this delicacy is in the form of a sandwich, and one of the best sandwich forms it can take is that of a po' boy. The pressed French bread, crispy fried soft-shell crab, and Cajun seasonings will deliver a memorable experience, whether for lunch or dinner or a decadent afternoon snack.

4 soft-shell crabs
1/2 cup whole milk
2 tablespoons Cajun seasoning
   or Old Bay Seasoning®
Juice of 1/2 a medium lemon
   or orange
1 large egg
1 cup cornmeal

1/2 cup olive oil, for frying
1 large clove garlic, finely
   chopped
1 loaf French bread or 2
   French baguettes, cut for 4
   sandwiches
2 teaspoons hot pepper sauce
   of your choice

Marinate the soft-shell crabs in milk, Cajun seasoning, and the lemon or orange juice for 30 minutes. Remove from the marinade and pat dry. Beat the egg into the marinade mixture. Dip the crab into the egg mixture and then into the cornmeal, covering both sides thoroughly.

In a sauté pan or iron skillet, heat the oil on medium heat and add in the garlic until oil begins to lightly smoke. Place the crabs in the pan, cooking each side approximately 5 minutes; reduce heat if the cornmeal begins to burn.

Butter each side of a French baguette. Sprinkle the inside top of baguettes with the hot pepper sauce. Place the cooked crabs into the sandwiches, and press into a pan under a heavy warm iron skillet, with foil on the top of the bread, for 3 minutes or until firm and toasted. Serve warm. Cajun mustard makes a healthy and delicious alternative to butter on the sandwich. *Makes 4 sandwiches.*

Florida Blackened Grouper Sandwich

This is the most famous (and most frequently ordered) of all Florida sandwiches, from Key West to Panama City, and could be considered the signature dish of the state. Grouper is Florida's most prized fish, and the best of these sandwiches are found near the Gulf and Atlantic beaches. Native Floridians know that it is a healthy and incredibly delicious alternative to hamburgers or fried grouper sandwiches. Blackened grouper sandwiches are always a great choice at the local bar, pub, or restaurant.

4 6-ounce fresh grouper fillets
2 tablespoons Blackening Spice Mix (see below)
1 tablespoon salted butter (1 tablespoon extra virgin olive oil may be substituted)
Juice of 1 medium lemon
4 medium Kaiser rolls

Mustard Yogurt Sauce, for tableside spreading (see below)
4 lettuce leaves
4 large tomatoes slices
Lemon wedges
1/2 large red onion, thinly sliced, for garnish

Coat a grouper fillet with blackening spice mix. Sauté with butter or olive oil on high heat in an iron skillet or on a hot grill; this should take approximately 4 minutes on each side. Squeeze lemon juice on each side of the fish during cooking. Toast the rolls and add a thin layer of mustard yogurt sauce (tartar sauce may be substituted), lettuce, and tomato. Add the fish to the rolls and serve hot, garnished with lemon wedges, sliced red onion, mustard yogurt sauce, and a side of chips or French fries. *Makes 4 sandwiches.*

Blackening Spice Mix

1 teaspoon garlic powder
1 teaspoon Spanish paprika
1 teaspoon ground black pepper

1 teaspoon cayenne pepper
1/2 teaspoon salt
1/2 teaspoon dry thyme
1/2 teaspoon dry mustard

Mix all ingredients and set aside.

Mustard Yogurt Sauce

1 tablespoon Dijon mustard
1 teaspoon whole-grain mus-
* tard*
1/2 cup low-fat yogurt
* (mayonnaise may be sub-*
* stituted)*

2 dashes hot pepper sauce of
* your choice*
1/3 teaspoon chopped dill
Salt and freshly ground pepper
* to taste*

Mix all the ingredients together and set aside in the refrigerator at least 15 minutes.

Tampa-style Cuban Sandwich

The Cuban sandwich is famous in Tampa, where they are purported to have been invented, not Cuba as some might think. It helps that Tampa has the nation's third largest Cuban population. Wherever you are from, you simply must have one! It's a simple sandwich to make, but no two sandwich shops or restaurants make them exactly the same, though most claim to have "The Best." The bread is the key—it must be fresh and toasted just right, not too crunchy nor too soft.

1 tablespoon mayonnaise	1/2 pound salami, sliced
1 tablespoon yellow mustard	1/2 pound boiled ham, sliced
Hot pepper sauce of your choice	1/2 pound pork shoulder or loin, sliced
Dash black pepper	1/2 pound sliced Swiss cheese, thinly sliced
2-foot loaf Cuban bread, cut in half and sliced length-wise	1/4 cup salted butter, melted
	4 lettuce leaves (optional)
1 deli pickle, thinly sliced	8 thin tomato slices (optional)

Mix the mayonnaise and mustard together with a dash of hot sauce and black pepper. Slather this mixture on both insides of the bread, and then add a row of deli pickle slices. Next lay down the salami, followed by the ham, then the pork, and finally the Swiss cheese on top. Cover the sandwich with the other half of the bread, brush the top and bottom of the bread with the melted butter and press for 5 minutes.* If desired, add lettuce and tomato after pressing for a "dressed" Cuban. *Makes 2 large or 4 small sandwiches.*

*A heavy hot iron skillet works well for pressing sandwiches at home. Press the sandwiches into a pan under a heavy warm iron skillet. Cover the top of sandwich with foil before pressing.

☜

Entrées

Stone Crab Claws

Stone crab claws are cooked immediately after they are caught, either on the boat or docks, as prescribed by Florida law. Therefore, to enjoy the flavor at its freshest, it is good to eat them near the source. All you have to do is put as many as you have in a big bowl, decide if you want them cold or warm, and enjoy! As a side note, only the largest claw is taken, and the crabs are then released back to the water. That makes the nature conservationists in us smile.

1/8 cup Dijon mustard
1/8 cup brown mustard
1 tablespoon mayonnaise
1 cup sour cream
2 medium lemons (cut into wedges)

5 pounds stone crab claws
Drawn butter*

Mix mustards, mayonnaise, sour cream, and 2 teaspoons of lemon juice together to make a dipping sauce. Serve stone crab claws with drawn butter, dipping sauce, lemon wedges, and several nutcrackers. A hammer or kitchen mallet can be used for cracking the claws. If the meal is a more elegant setting, pre-cracking is recommended. Light beer, dry white wine, and Champagne are all wonderful accompaniments to stone crab claws. *Makes 5 servings.*

*Drawn butter refers to butter that has been slowly heated in a saucepan with the fatty solids skimmed from the top. The result is a clear, "drawn" butter that is typically served with fresh seafood for dipping.

ᴄ🙰◯

Blue Crab Fest

A blue crab fest is arguably the most traditional and enjoyable of all Florida culinary activities. A crab fest is not a simple dinner, it's an event! Don't make any plans for the day, as they will take hours to eat. The work required to get the meat is a small price to pay for the rewarding taste of this prized shellfish.

4 12-ounce cans cheap domestic beer such as Bud Lite or Natural Light (water can be substituted)
1/4 cup white vinegar
1/2 cup Old Bay Seasoning® or other crab boil seasoning

1 medium head garlic, separated and peeled
4 dozen medium or large live blue crabs
Drawn butter*
2 medium lemons (cut into wedges)

Serve this event outside unless you are planning to move. Whatever surface you choose, cover it with plenty of newspapers (and have more standing by) to soak up the juices. Having this event outside allows you to hose the area down after the feast is over. You need nutcrackers and/or hammers to crack the claws, and small forks to get the meat out. Have plenty of large bowls for empty shells, as well as a big supply of napkins or paper towels.

In a very large pot or crab boiler, pour in the beer or water and the vinegar. Bring to a boil, then add the Old Bay Seasoning and garlic. Allow liquid to come to a full boil. Add the live crabs to the pot (not all of the crabs have to be submerged, as the upper layers can steam). Cover and boil for 10 minutes. Serve the crabs hot or cold with drawn butter and lemon wedges. Light American beer is the perfect accompaniment, but any refreshing beverage will do, as the star of this meal is the crab! *Yields 6–8 sesrvings.*

Tip: A small claw tool works better than a fork for extracting meat from the claws and body of blue crabs.

*Drawn butter refers to butter that has been slowly heated in a saucepan with the fatty solids skimmed from the top. The result is a clear, "drawn" butter that is typically served with fresh seafood for dipping.

Grouper with Orange Sauce

This dish is a marriage between the quintessential Florida fish and the most famous Florida fruit. Grouper and oranges are kings of their respective bounty realms. This recipe makes a wonderfully light and tangy fish that goes well with numerous other foods, from a tangy Caesar salad to a spicy salsa or orange zest hushpuppies. Rice is perhaps the best starch option as it blends well with the orange sauce.

4 8-ounce grouper fillets
3/4 cup freshly squeezed
   orange juice
1/2 teaspoon salt
1/2 teaspoon freshly ground
   black pepper
2 tablespoons salted butter
2 teaspoons extra virgin olive
   oil

4 tablespoons shallots,
   chopped
1/2 cup dry white wine
Juice of 1 medium lemon
1/4 cup water
2 tablespoons cornstarch
3 teaspoons sherry
Lemon and orange slices for
   garnish

Marinate the grouper for 30 minutes in 1/4 cup of the orange juice.

Place the fillets on a broiling pan. Lightly coat with salt and pepper and then pour the orange juice marinade over the fish. Broil for 10 minutes or until grouper is opaque white throughout.

Meanwhile, melt butter and olive oil over medium-low heat in a saucepan. Add shallots and sauté until caramelized. Raise heat to medium-high and add wine and cook for 2 minutes to steam out the alcohol. Add remaining orange and lemon juices; then reduce heat to medium. While the sauce simmers, mix the water with the cornstarch in a separate cup. Slowly pour into the sauce, stirring constantly with a whisk. Slowly stir in the sherry to finish the sauce. Reduce until sauce clings to a metal spoon.

Plate the fillets and serve with orange sauce drizzled over the top. Add lemon and orange slices as a garnish. This dish goes very well with both Riesling and Gewurztraminer, as the crispness of these white wines complement the bold sweetness of the sauce. *Yields 4 8-ounce entrée servings.*

☞

Costa Rican–style Grouper al Ajillo

Grouper al Ajillo is prominent on menus in Costa Rica and throughout Latin America; however, the preparation technique and the ingredients are a perfect match for the Florida climate and style of cooking. In Costa Rica, white lake perch or sea bass are commonly used, but we have found that grouper has a texture and flavor that truly complements the Florida "al ajillo" style.

2 pounds fresh grouper fillets
1 large head garlic, peeled and
 finely chopped
Juice of 1 medium lemon (lime
 juice may be substituted)
2 tablespoons salted butter

4 tablespoon extra virgin olive
 oil
4 teaspoons fresh cilantro,
 chopped

Coat both sides of the grouper fillets with half of the chopped garlic. Place in shallow dish and pour lemon juice over the fillets. Cover and refrigerate for 1 hour.

In a large skillet, melt the butter and olive oil over low heat. Add the rest of the garlic and adjust heat to medium high. Sauté until the garlic begins to brown, and then add fish to the skillet and sauté 5 minutes on each side. To finish the dish, sprinkle cilantro over the fillets and transfer to a serving platter. *Yields 4 8-ounce entrée servings.*

Serve with a starch such as rice, potatoes, or yucca. For an accompanying wine, try an Italian Orvieto Classico or a French Pouilly-Fumé.

⋘⋙

Salted Red Snapper

Although originally an Italian dish, salted fish is a natural fit for Florida when one considers the bounty of fish from the state's coastal waters. It may be due to the fact that, like Italy, Florida has water on three sides. Salted Red Snapper is not difficult to make, but your guests will think you have become a master chef when it is presented and "cracked" at the table.

1 sprig of rosemary
4 tablespoons extra virgin olive oil
2 pounds fresh, whole red snapper with scales still on
Juice of 1 medium lemon
Juice of 1 medium orange

4 pounds sea salt (this coarse salt is available in specialty grocery stores; kosher salt may be substituted)
1/4 cup all-purpose flour
1/2 cup water

Place the olive oil and rosemary in a covered container. Set aside for at least an hour to allow the flavor of the rosemary to infuse the olive oil. Then rub the outside skin and the cleaned belly of the fish (with head on) with 1 tablespoon of the rosemary-infused olive oil. Thinly slice the lemons and oranges, placing half of each into the belly of the fish. Add the rosemary and gently squeeze the fish shut.

In a long, narrow baking pan, put down a thin layer of salt, and set the fish on top. Pour the remaining salt over the fish, making sure to cover entirely. Mix the flour thoroughly into the water, and pour the mixture over the salted fish, being careful not to expose the fish. Bake at 400°F for 45 minutes.

Remove the fish from the oven and let cool for 10 minutes. Then crack the salt casing with the back of a heavy knife. Carefully peel the salt and skin away (they should come off the meat together). Remove the fish from the salt casing carefully and serve with the remaining olive oil and lemon wedges. The fish will not be too salty; it will be tender and nicely seasoned. In keeping with the Italian tradition, include a bottle of Pinot Grigio. The crispness of this white wine goes perfectly with the salted fish. *Yields 4 8-ounce entrée servings.*

Note: Red snapper is used in this dish for its scales, which should be left on, and for the sweet quality of the meat, which is sealed in by the coating of sea salt. If red snapper is not available, mangrove snapper may also be used.

Pasta with Florida Shellfish in Tomato Cream

Seafood pasta is perhaps one of the most common pasta dishes found in Florida, and when it is done well you can easily understand why. It really is a must for any cookbook on Florida food. This recipe is relatively easy to prepare and portion variations can be accomplished with little or no trouble. We hope you enjoy the experience of having delectable seafood pasta at home with family and friends.

4 tablespoons shallots, chopped

2 tablespoon extra virgin olive oil

1/2 pound small bay scallops

1/2 pound fresh small or medium shrimp, cleaned and deveined

Salt and freshly ground black pepper to taste

3 cups tomato sauce (see below)

1/2 cup heavy whipping cream

1 pound farfalle pasta, cooked according to package instructions

Parmesan cheese for topping

In a medium saucepan, add the shallots to heated olive oil and cook over medium heat until caramelized. Add the scallops, shrimp, salt, and pepper, and sauté approximately 4 minutes. Add tomato sauce and simmer over medium-low heat for approximately 20 minutes. Reduce heat to low and slowly stir in the cream. Continue to heat for 2–3 minutes. Taste and season as appropriate with salt and pepper. Serve over cooked pasta with grated parmesan at the table. *Yields 4 entrée servings.*

Tomato Sauce

2 large cloves garlic, finely
chopped
1 1/2 teaspoons extra virgin
olive oil
1 tablespoon fresh parsley,
chopped
1 tablespoon fresh basil,
chopped

1 teaspoon fresh oregano,
chopped
1 bay leaf
2 14-ounce cans whole peeled
tomatoes, pureed in
blender

In a sauce pan, sauté the garlic in olive oil over a medium-high heat for 5 minutes. Add the herbs and stir for 1 minute. Pour in pureed tomatoes and bring to boil. Reduce heat to simmer, cover, and cook for 50–60 minutes. Remove bay leaf prior to serving. *Yields 3 cups of sauce.*

⌬

Linguini with Classic Clam Sauce

Clam sauce is more than a comfort food: it has become a food staple of life. It's not always very sexy (though it can be), but it is healthy, hearty, and without parallel for comfort and quality. Here we present two styles, both of which make a lovely dinner for two!

2 teaspoons salted butter
2 tablespoons extra virgin
   olive oil
4 large cloves garlic, finely
   chopped
1/4 teaspoon medium-heat red
   chili pepper, finely minced
1 dozen fresh littleneck clams,
   soaked in cold water for 5
   minutes
1 6.5-ounce can minced clams,
   strained; reserve juice
1 cup dry white wine

2 tablespoons fresh parsley,
   chopped
1 tablespoon fresh basil,
   chopped
Juice of 1 small lemon
Salt and fresh ground black
   pepper to taste
Lemon wedges, for garnish
Parmesan cheese, thinly
   shaved, for garnish
8 ounces linguini, cooked
   according to package
   instructions

In a medium saucepan, melt butter and olive oil together over low heat. Adjust heat to medium and add the garlic and chili pepper. Sauté until garlic toasts to a golden brown. Add fresh and canned clams, sautéing for approximately 5 minutes. Add the wine and cook for 2 minutes to steam out the alcohol. Pour in the reserved clam juice and cook for an additional 5 minutes. Add fresh herbs and lemon juice and simmer on low heat for 30 minutes. Taste and season as appropriate with salt and pepper. Combine the pasta and the sauce; serve with the lemon wedges and shaved parmesan. *Yields 2 generous entrée portions.*

Cream-style Clam Sauce

2 tablespoon all-purpose flour
1/4 cup whole milk
1 tablespoon salted butter

Prepare Classic Clam Sauce as above. In a drinking glass, beat flour and milk together with a fork to dissolve flour. Pour mixture into Classic Clam Sauce, simmering an additional 10 minutes. Melt the butter into the sauce immediately before serving. Garnish with lemon wedges and parmesan and serve over linguini as above. *Yields 2 generous entrée portions.*

Pop's Red Clam Sauce

This recipe helped to launch a culinary life. I used to spend long Saturdays shopping for the freshest ingredients with my father. It was the perfect day to him, as he comes from a long line of sailors and is always more comfortable when the sea is involved. Pop's red clam sauce was, and is, a labor of love. Like our classic clam sauce it is healthy, hearty, and a winner for comfort and quality.

4 tablespoons extra virgin olive oil

8 large cloves garlic, finely chopped

1 teaspoon medium-heat red chili pepper, finely minced

1/2 cup scallions

4 dozen fresh clams, soaked in cold water for 5 minutes

2 6.5-ounce cans minced clams, strained; reserve juice

4 14-ounce cans seeded tomatoes, pureed

3 tablespoons fresh parsley, chopped

4 tablespoon fresh basil, chopped

1/2 cup Chianti

Salt and freshly ground black pepper to taste

32 ounces linguini, cooked according to package instructions

Parmesan cheese, thinly shaved for garnish

In a large saucepot, heat olive oil over medium high heat and sauté the garlic and chili pepper until garlic toasts to a golden brown. Incorporate scallions and fresh and canned clams, sautéing for approximately 5 minutes. Add the pureed tomatoes and half of the parsley and basil, and then simmer for 30 minutes. Raise heat back to medium, add the Chianti and cook for 3 minutes to steam out the alcohol. Pour in the reserved clam juice and remaining basil and parsley, and cook for an additional 10 minutes. Taste and season as appropriate with salt and pepper. Toss with prepared linguini and serve with shaved parmesan cheese tableside. *Yields 8 entrée portions.*

∝∾

Key West Pork Tenderloin

This recipe joins two of the prominent Caribbean flavors together for a hot, sweet and sour dish that is perfect for a summer barbecue or a weekday dinner. You will find the heat and smokiness of the habanero pepper to be a perfect match for the sticky sweetness of the mangos, creating a sultry tropical masterpiece accented perfectly by the tanginess of the limes.

1 medium Florida mango, peeled and cut into quarter-inch pieces*

2 large cloves garlic, finely chopped

1 to 2 habanero peppers, finely chopped

Juice of 2 medium limes

Juice of 1 medium orange

1 teaspoon fresh ground black pepper

2-pound pork tenderloin, whole

Add mango to a large marinade dish with the garlic and habaneros. If you like very hot food, use both habanero peppers. If you prefer your world a little cooler, use only half of a habanero pepper. Yes, the peppers are that hot! Add in the juice of the limes and the orange. Sprinkle in the fresh ground pepper. Do not add salt. Roll the pork tenderloin in the marinade until completely coated. Cover and refrigerate 4–24 hours. Rotate the pork occasionally so that all sides have a chance to soak in the marinade.

Grill the pork over a very high heat. The marinade will crust over as the pork finishes, enhancing the smoky flavors from the habanero pepper. Cook the pork medium to medium-well (a light center pink is good on high quality tenderloins.) Serve with a light salad and fruit tart for dessert.

A bold Riesling wine such as a German Mosel or light Caribbean beer will match the heat with the sweet and sour flavors. *Yields 6 entrée portions.*

*How to peel a mango: With a sharp paring knife, slice the skin off the mango, being careful not to slice away fruit unnecessarily. After skinning the mango, use the knife to slice off pieces of the fruit. Do not cut into the seed, which feels fibrous under the knife. Good luck and have fun!

Pan-fried Soft-shell Crab with Homemade Cole Slaw

This is a wonderfully light and tangy dish that can be used for any number of occasions. The best occasion, perhaps, is finding these soft-shelled delicacies. The presentation is impressive and will make for a charming and colorful plate, with the crabs arranged as succulent orange flower petals upon a soft bed of cabbage and herbs. By using buttermilk and yogurt instead of cream and mayonnaise, you can create a healthy yet luscious meal.

4 medium-size soft-shell crabs   1/4 teaspoon salt
1 cup buttermilk   1/4 teaspoon freshly ground
2 medium lemons   black pepper
2 large eggs   4 teaspoons olive oil
1/2 cup cornmeal   2 large cloves garlic, finely

Marinate the soft-shell crabs in buttermilk and the juice of half a lemon for 30 minutes. Remove from the marinade and pat dry. Beat the eggs into the marinade mixture. Spread combined cornmeal, salt, and pepper onto a plate. Dip the crab into the egg mixture, then into the cornmeal, covering both sides thoroughly.

In an iron skillet, heat the oil over medium heat and add the garlic. Once the oil begins to smoke, add the crabs. Cook on each side approximately 5 minutes. Reduce heat if the cornmeal begins to burn. Serve immediately, placed at a diagonal on top of a mound of coleslaw. *Yields 4 servings.*

Cole Slaw

1/4 head white cabbage
1 tablespoon plain low-fat
   yogurt
2 teaspoon tarragon vinegar
   (cider vinegar can be substituted)
1/2 teaspoon mayonnaise

1 teaspoon Dijon mustard
1 1/2 teaspoons cilantro
1/4 teaspoon celery seed
Salt and fresh ground black
   pepper to taste

Julienne the cabbage and put into a large mixing bowl. Add yogurt, vinegar, mayonnaise, mustard, cilantro, and celery seed. Toss well and season with salt and pepper to taste. *Yields 4 servings.*

Florida Lobster Ravioli in Sage Butter

This luxurious dish can be time-consuming to prepare, but the rewards are an overwhelming delight for the senses. Note that you need a pasta machine for this recipe. When the ravioli is tossed with melted butter and fresh sage, a few simple ingredients are transformed into an extraordinary masterpiece. Each bite will slowly melt in your mouth, creating a unique taste sensation. But don't take our word for it—experience the joy for yourself.

Ravioli Filling

1/4 pound Florida lobster, delicately chopped (Maine lobster or lump crab meat can be substituted)	1 large egg
	1/8 teaspoon nutmeg
	1/4 teaspoon salt
	1/4 teaspoon pepper
1/2 cup ricotta cheese	
1/2 cup parmesan cheese, grated	

Mix all ingredients and chill while making pasta.

Pasta
2 cups all-purpose flour
2 large eggs

Sauce
4 tablespoons salted butter
1/8 cup fresh sage, thinly sliced

On a clean counter, make a mound of flour. Form a well in the center with your fingers, so that the mound resembles a volcano. Crack the eggs into the center and use a fork to gently beat them, slowly pulling flour into the center of the well. When dough becomes a solid mass, pick it up and discard all leftover flour. Knead for 4–6 minutes on a lightly floured surface (using clean flour), until dough becomes smooth. Cut off a quarter of the dough, setting the rest aside in a cheesecloth or slightly dampened dishtowel. Roll out the dough in a pasta machine, progressing to the second to last notch. Lay pasta strips on counter and place 1 teaspoon of the lobster/ricotta mixture at 2-inch intervals. Lay second pasta sheet on top and press down in between the filling. Cut with pizza cutter and fork all sides.

Gently place ravioli in a pot of boiling water and cook for 3 minutes. Meanwhile, melt butter in a large sauté pan. Add sage and keep heat on low. Drain ravioli in a colander and toss with butter sauce in the frying pan. Serve immediately, garnished with grated parmesan. *Yields 4 entrée portions.*

Maryland-style Crab Cakes

While the title may say Maryland, crab cakes are common at most Florida restaurants, as well as in many homes. It can be argued that Florida blue crabs are better than those of our Northern friends anyway. Serve crab cakes as a main course or as a snack. It is possible to freeze any leftover cakes for individual meals. Most importantly, don't look for a special occasion—have them for any reason!

2 large eggs, beaten
1 large clove garlic, finely chopped
1 teaspoon Dijon mustard
1 teaspoon whole-grain mustard
1 teaspoon Worcestershire Sauce
1 1/2 teaspoons fresh Italian parsley, finely chopped
1 1/2 teaspoons fresh basil, finely chopped
1/2 cup plus 2 tablespoons fine Italian-style bread crumbs

1 tablespoon lemon juice
Pinch of red or cayenne pepper
1/4 teaspoon salt
1/4 teaspoon fresh ground black pepper
1 pound cleaned blue crab meat
1 tablespoon extra virgin olive oil
1 teaspoon salted butter

Combine all ingredients except crab meat, olive oil, and butter in a mixing bowl. Carefully fold in the crab meat, trying not to break it up. Form mixture into handful-size balls and then flatten out to cakes approximately 3 inches in diameter.

Heat olive oil and butter in a skillet or sauté pan over medium heat. Cook the crab cakes until each side is golden brown. Remove and place on paper towels to drain. Serve warm with a mustard yogurt sauce (see p. 126). *Yields 4 appetizer or 2 entrée portions.*

Dixie Fried Fish

For those living in northern Florida, especially in rural portions of the Panhandle, Southern culture remains the predominant influence over cooking styles. Over the years, catfish and other fish lacking respect in other parts of the state have developed a reputation in the north as a delicious, inexpensive treat. Dixie fried fish is our homage to the Southern roots of north Florida, where fried fish, hush puppies, cheese grits, and cole slaw make a feast fit for a watermelon queen.

4 8-ounce fresh catfish fillets
  (whitefish or tilapia may
  be substituted)
1 tablespoon canola oil
2 tablespoons warm water

1/4 cup all-purpose flour
1/2 teaspoon salt
1/4 teaspoon black pepper
1 egg white
Canola oil for frying

Rinse and dry the fish. Mix oil and warm water together in a small bowl. In a medium bowl, combine flour, salt, and pepper. Using a wire whisk, beat the oil and water into dry mixture until it is smooth. Let stand for 15 minutes at room temperature. Beat egg white in a glass bowl until stiff peaks form. Just before frying, add egg white into the batter and gently fold in until incorporated. In a heavy frying pan, heat 1 inch of oil over high heat. The oil is ready when a drop of water sizzles and crackles. Completely coat 2 of the fillets in the batter. Gently place the fillets in the oil. Fry until golden brown, approximately 3–4 minutes on each side. Remove fillets from oil, and place on a plate covered in paper towels to soak up excess grease. Repeat the process with remaining fillets. Serve immediately with your favorite Southern side dishes. *Yields 4 servings.*

Florida Jambalaya with Grits

Borrowed from our Cajun and Creole friends in Louisiana, this version of jambalaya has a true Southern twist and uses grits instead of rice. The grits actually add a creamy lusciousness that rice cannot, and the slight hint of corn flavor works perfectly. It takes time to prepare this dish, but your efforts will be well rewarded. If you don't have a crowd to serve, you will have leftovers to enjoy for days.

1 tablespoon salted butter
1 large red onion, thinly
   chopped
4 scallions, thinly chopped
1 large green bell pepper,
   chopped
3 large cloves garlic, minced
2 bay leaves
1 jalapeño pepper, finely
   chopped
2 tablespoons Creole seasoning
1/2 teaspoon cayenne pepper
2 tablespoons fresh Italian
   parsley, chopped
1 tablespoon fresh thyme,
   chopped
1 tablespoon fresh oregano,
   chopped
2 red chili peppers, finely
   chopped (fresh or dry)

1 tablespoon tomato paste
1 pound andouille sausage,
   sliced (Polish kielbasa can
   be substituted when
   andouille sausage is not
   available)
1 pound boiled ham, cubed
1/2 pound fresh medium Gulf
   shrimp, peeled and
   deveined
1/4 pound scallops
4 cups chicken stock
3 cups low-fat milk
1 14.5-ounce can diced tomatoes
2 cups stone-ground grits
Voodoo pepper sauce to taste
Salt and freshly ground pepper
   to taste

Melt butter in a large, heavy pot over medium-high heat. Add red onion, 3 scallions, bell pepper, garlic, bay leaves, jalapeño, Creole seasoning, cayenne pepper, parsley, thyme, oregano, and chili peppers. Cover and cook until vegetables are tender, stirring occasionally, about 15 minutes. Mix in tomato paste. Add sausage, ham, shrimp, scallops, chicken stock, milk, tomatoes, and grits. Bring mixture to simmer. Reduce heat to

low; cover, and cook until grits are very tender, stirring occasionally, about 1 hour. Add pepper sauce, salt, and pepper to
taste. Garnish with remaining scallion and serve in bowls.
Makes 6 entrée portions.

Shrimp Scampi Pizza

Too often, pizza is ordered for delivery or takeout, leading to a repetition of the same ingredients and styles. However, pizza is easy enough to make at home. Once you learn to make the dough, it is almost as fast as waiting for delivery. Homemade pizzas can also be a great party theme, where a variety of ingredients is presented for each guest to prepare his or her own individual pie. Kids will especially enjoy the chance to make their own special pizza. We've included a favorite recipe here, Shrimp Scampi Pizza, but feel free to try your own combinations: Mexican, Thai, Italian, Salmon and Goat Cheese, or even Indian-style! Think of the dough as a blank canvas and let your imagination run wild.

Pizza Dough

2 1/4 cups all-purpose flour
1/4 ounce package fast-acting
    yeast
1/2 teaspoon salt
1 teaspoon granulated sugar
1/2 cup milk and 1/4 cup
    water, mixed and heated
    until hot to touch

1 tablespoon extra virgin olive
    oil (added to hot
    milk/water mixture)

Sift together dry ingredients. Incorporate the liquid and mix with a fork or your hands until a loose dough is formed. Turn out dough on lightly floured surface and knead for 5 minutes, until the dough is soft, smooth, and pliable. Place dough in a lightly oiled bowl, cover tightly with plastic wrap, and let it sit until it has doubled in size. This will take approximately 1 hour.

Scampi Pizza Topping

1 tablespoon salted butter

5 teaspoons extra virgin olive oil

4 large cloves garlic, minced

1 pound fresh small shrimp, peeled and deveined

1 tablespoon fresh parsley, roughly chopped

1 tablespoon fresh basil, roughly chopped

1 tablespoon dry white wine (Sauvignon or Chenin Blanc)

Juice of 1 medium lemon

2 teaspoons cornmeal

1 1/2 cups high quality mozzarella cheese, shredded

1 1/2 tablespoons parmesan cheese

1/2 teaspoon salt

Freshly ground black pepper

In a sauté pan on medium-high heat, melt butter into 2 teaspoons of the olive oil. Add minced garlic and sauté until garlic becomes soft and translucent. Add shrimp and chopped herbs. Add wine and lemon juice; let alcohol steam out for 10 seconds, and then remove from heat.

Knead dough for 1 minute, and then roll out dough on a floured surface to desired shape and thickness. Carefully transfer dough to a heated pizza stone or baking pan, pulling back into shape. To prevent sticking, sprinkle 2 teaspoons of cornmeal on stone/pan before transfer. Brush dough liberally with the remaining olive oil. Top with scampi mixture, then the mozzarella and parmesan cheeses. Pour any remaining liquid from cooking the scampi over the pizza. If necessary, fold the edges of the dough up slightly to form a crust. Season with salt and pepper. Cook for approximately 10 minutes at 425°F. Cut with a sharp pizza cutter and enjoy! *Yields 3–4 entrée portions.*

Note: A typical pizza dough batch will make 1 12x18-inch pizza or 2 9-inch pizzas. Alternatively, the dough can be split multiple times for appetizer-size pizzettas. The scampi recipe above allows for 1 batch of pizza dough.

Grecian Urn Burger

Beef ranks as one of Florida's top agricultural products. Florida is a top producer of beef east of the Mississippi river, and cattle have been raised here since the earliest Spanish settlers. It is therefore a natural product to consider when planning for meals representative of the state.

Here we have mixed a bit of lamb with beef to provide a delicious and extremely flavorful burger that gives it a "Grecian" taste—with a tip of the Florida hat to our Greek friends in Tarpon Springs. The burger is an "urn" that hides the cheese, leaving you wondering what a "real" cheeseburger is: should the cheese be in the middle or on top? You decide.

1 1/2 pounds lean ground beef	*1 clove garlic, finely chopped*
1/2 pound lean ground lamb	*1 teaspoon salt and pepper*
1 tablespoon chopped fresh parsley	*2 tablespoons extra virgin olive oil*
1 tablespoon chopped fresh dill	*6 tablespoons blue cheese*

Combine all ingredients, excluding 1 tablespoon olive oil and the blue cheese, together in a bowl and mix thoroughly. Split the mixture into 6 equal parts and form into large meatballs. Make a hole in each meatball using the back of a small spoon or your thumb. Put a tablespoon of blue cheese in each meatball hole, then re-form the meatball. Form the burger patties by flattening the meatballs until they are approximately a half-inch-thick and uniformly round. Set aside.

The burgers can be cooked on the stove or on the grill. If cooking on a stove put a tablespoon of olive oil in a heavy skillet or sauté pan. Bring to medium heat. Cook the burgers on one side until juices begin to show on the patty surface. Then flip the burger, lower the heat to medium-low, and cook until juices again appear. Remove the burgers from the heat. This will provide a medium-rare to medium burger. The same technique can be used on a grill, but in that case no oil is required.

Serve the burgers with fresh tomatoes, red onions, and a side of either coleslaw or fritters. A glass of red wine would best complement the meal. To save time, these burger patties can be made a few hours ahead of time. *Serves 6.*

Caribbean-style Beef and Sugar Cane Stew in Coconut Milk

Sugar cane and beef represent large sectors of the Florida agricultural output. Here we have combined those two commodities with the flavorful sweet jerk seasonings borrowed from some of Florida's neighbors. While sweet beef may seem strange, give it a try and you will develop an appreciation for it—as well as the various cultural influences on Florida.

2 tablespoons extra virgin olive oil
2 cloves whole garlic
8 medium carrots, cut into 2-inch pieces
8 small Spanish onions
1 bay leaf
5 pounds beef bottom round roast or London broil, cut into 2-inch cubes
3 feet of fresh Florida sugar cane, cut into 2-inch pieces
1 can regular coconut milk

1 can light coconut milk
1 cup low-fat plain yogurt
1 teaspoon nutmeg
1/2 teaspoon mace
1 teaspoon cumin
2 whole cinnamon sticks
1 teaspoon whole cloves
1 teaspoon cayenne pepper
1/4 cup sea salt
2 tablespoons freshly ground black pepper
1 large lemon, cut into 8 slices

In a large Dutch oven or stew pot, add the olive oil, garlic, carrots, onions, and bay leaf and sauté over medium heat until the onions are translucent. Add the beef and sugar cane and sauté until the meat is browned on all sides. Add the remaining ingredients and bring to a low boil. Lower the heat to medium-low and simmer for 2–4 hours. Serve with white or brown rice. *Yields 10–12 servings.*

Rice
3 cups water
1 cup chicken or beef stock
2 cups white or brown rice
1 tablespoon salt

To prepare the rice:
Add the water, stock, and rice, along with the salt, to a large pot. Cover and bring to a boil. Stir the rice and reduce heat to low; stir until the boiling subsides. Let simmer about 20 minutes or until all the water is gone and the rice is fluffy. Serve warm.

24-Hour Yogurt-marinated Beef Roast

Yogurt is wonderful medium in which to marinate virtually any type of meat. It works especially well with beef because the active cultures and enzymes work with the flavors you add to tenderize and flavor the meat. Marinate the meat over night and you will taste the difference immediately; it will have a richer flavor and more tender texture.

4 cloves garlic, chopped
1 cup low-fat plain yogurt
1/4 cup extra virgin olive oil
Fresh ground black pepper
Juice of half a large lemon

4–5 pounds bottom round,
London broil, or butt
roast
1 tablespoon salt

In a large bowl or marinating dish, mix the garlic, yogurt, olive oil, black pepper, and lemon juice together. Place the beef in the dish and cover completely with the marinade mixture. Cover with plastic wrap and place in the refrigerator over night.

Preheat the oven to 400°F. To prepare the meat for cooking, rub the salt evenly into the beef. Place it in the oven and cook at 400°F for 30 minutes. Then reduce the heat to 350°F and cook for an additional 30 minutes. This should provide a medium-rare to medium roast. Slice thinly and server with potatoes, couscous, or any other hearty starch dish. A glass of red Spanish wine would be a great accompaniment, as would a fresh salad of greens and tomatoes with oil and vinegar. Enjoy this easy yet effective technique for marinating meats— try it on all your favorites. *Makes 8 servings.*

Super Fast, Super Good Turkey

How to cook a turkey? There are nearly as many ways as there are people who cook them. You can fry, boil, bake, and smoke it; you can cook it covered or uncovered, quickly or for hours and hours. This recipe is a tried and true way to get a delicious and juicy turkey in a relatively short period of time with a minimum of preparation and equipment. This works great if you need the oven for other things.

4 large sprigs rosemary
1/4 cup extra virgin olive oil
1 medium turkey (10–12 pounds)
1 medium yellow onion, cut in half

2 large lemons, halved
2 tablespoons salt
1 tablespoon freshly ground black pepper

Soak the rosemary in the olive oil for at least 1 hour. Preheat the oven to 450°F. After rinsing the turkey with clean water and patting dry, rub down with the rosemary-infused olive oil, salt, and pepper. Carefully put the remaining rosemary sprigs under the skin of the turkey at the breast. Place the onions in the cavity of the turkey. Squeeze the lemons over the turkey and place one of the remaining lemon halves in the turkey cavity and the other under the skin flap at the neck of the turkey. Place the turkey on a roasting rack and place in the oven. Cook for 45 minutes at 450°F, then reduce the heat to 350°F and cook for 2 hours and 15 minutes. Use a meat thermometer to make sure the turkey has reached a temperature of 185°F; obtain the reading by putting the thermometer about an inch into the thigh. *Yields 8 servings.*

Stuffed Tomatoes

Stuffed tomatoes make a great vegetarian alternative for those limiting meat and seafood consumption. They also work well as a side dish. The mushrooms provide a firm texture that is both satisfying and delicious.

2 tablespoons extra virgin
   olive oil
1 pound white mushrooms,
   chopped into small pieces
1 cup Spanish onions, finely
   chopped
2 cloves garlic, minced
1 teaspoon fresh thyme, finely
   chopped
1 tablespoon fresh parsley,
   finely chopped

1/4 cup vegetable or chicken
   stock
1 cup Italian-style bread
   crumbs
6 medium beefsteak tomatoes,
   with the centers cored out
   and discarded
6 slices provolone cheese

Preheat oven to 350°F. Heat olive oil in large skillet over medium heat. Sauté mushrooms, onions, and garlic for 5–7 minutes until soft and onions become translucent. Stir in herbs, stock, and bread crumbs. Remove from heat and let sit for 5 minutes. If desired, additional bread crumbs can be added for a more robust stuffing. Spoon the stuffing evenly into the 6 tomatoes. Bake tomatoes for 20 minutes and remove from oven. Adjust oven to broil, top each tomato with a slice of provolone, and broil until cheese is bubbly and golden brown. *Makes 3 entrée portions or 6 side vegetable portions.*

Sides

Grits, grits, grits!

Grits are a true Southern favorite. Many people who are not from the South do not like or understand grits, though there are exceptions. To those who have discovered the joys of smooth, creamy grits, welcome to the American South! The Northern dislike comes from a misconception that all grits are instant, wet, and served with sugar and too much margarine. This is where the confusion begins. Would rice be so popular if it was only served with butter? The same can be asked of pasta or potatoes. Grits are in fact, like most starches, a wonderful base for flavor and color. Try to avoid instant grits, and experiment with using chicken or vegetable stock instead of water. Use grits rather than rice, fry it, just try it, and not just for breakfast!

Classic Southern Grits

1 tablespoon salted butter
1 cup regular grits
1 cup chicken stock (vegetable
   stock may be substituted)
1 cup water

1 tablespoon salt
Freshly ground black pepper
   to taste
Hot pepper sauce of your
   choice (optional)

In a medium-size saucepan, melt the butter. Add the grits, stirring until all the grits have been coated. Add the chicken stock and bring to a boil. Add half the water and lower to a simmer, stirring often. Simmer for ten minutes, then as the grits begin to thicken, add the rest of the water and continue to stir. Remove from the heat and add the salt and pepper. Serve with hot pepper sauce if desired. *Yields 4 servings.*

Note: If you are cooking with stone-ground grits, more liquid as well as more cooking time will be needed. Adjust the proportions to 3 cups of liquid per cup of stone-ground grits. While the stone-ground variety takes from 25–35 minutes to cook, the unrivaled rich taste and creamy texture will be well worth the time and effort.

Cheese Grits

1 tablespoon salted butter	*1/3 cup cheddar cheese, grated*
1 cup regular grits	*1/2 teaspoon salt*
1 cup chicken stock	*Freshly ground black pepper*
1 cup water	*to taste*
1/4 cup Monterey jack cheese,	*Hot pepper sauce of your*
grated	*choice (optional)*

In a hot medium-size saucepot, melt butter. Add the grits, stirring until all the grits have been coated. Pour in the stock and bring to a boil. Add half the water and lower to a simmer, stirring often. As the grits begin to thicken, add the rest of the water and continue to stir. Once grits have thickened (about 10 minutes), slowly stir in the cheeses. Remove from the heat and add the salt and pepper. Serve with your favorite hot pepper sauce on the side. *Yields 4 side dishes.*

Serve in a bowl or as a side dish with eggs, fish, or fried green tomatoes.

Spicy Jalapeño Grits

To funk it up a bit!

1 tablespoon salted butter	*1/4 cup Monterey jack cheese*
1 jalapeño pepper, seeded and	*(optional)*
finely diced	*1 tablespoon salt*
1 cup regular grits	*Freshly ground black pepper*
1 cup chicken stock	*to taste*
1 cup water	

In a hot medium-size saucepot, add the butter and then sauté half of the jalapeño pepper for 3 minutes. Then add the grits, stirring until all the grits have been coated. Add the stock and bring to a boil. Add half the water and lower to a simmer, stirring often. As the grits begin to thicken (about 10 minutes), add the rest of the water and continue to stir. Stir in the other half of the chopped jalapeño pepper. Once grits have been reduced to desired thickness and are tender, slowly stir in the cheese. Remove from the heat and add the salt, pepper, and pepper sauce. *Yields 4 servings.*

Grilled or Fried Grits

Heavenly for breakfast or dinner with fish or steak!

Prepare cheese grits as above, substituting 4 ounces plain cream cheese for the cheddar and Monterey jack cheeses. When the grits are done, pour into baking pan and spread evenly until smooth, approximately 3/4 inch thick. Let cool and refrigerate for at least 2 hours. Slice into wedges. Carefully remove from baking pan and either grill or sauté in butter on each side, until a golden crust forms. Simply delicious! *Yields 4 servings.*

❧

Fried Green Tomatoes

The rest of the United States discovered this dish watching them lovingly made at the Whistle Stop Café in the movie Fried Green Tomatoes. Floridians knew the dish much earlier and derive great pleasure from this acidic yet luscious fried food. Even children who claim not to like tomatoes (the red ones), will be enthralled by this tasty fried fruit/vegetable morsel. For a real Southern experience, serve with jalapeño cheese grits and sweet tea.

1 cup all-purpose flour
1 teaspoon cayenne pepper
1/2 teaspoon salt
1 cup whole milk
2 large eggs
3/4 cup fine Italian-style
*   bread crumbs*

4 medium-size fresh, firm
*   green tomatoes, cut into*
*   quarter-inch round slices*
1/2 cup vegetable or canola
*   oil, for cooking*

In 3 separate bowls prepare the following:
Flour, cayenne pepper, and salt, combined
Milk and eggs, beaten together
Bread crumbs

Dredge tomato slices through flour mixture; shake off excess ingredients, then dredge through egg/milk mixture, again shaking off excess mixture. Then coat the tomatoes with the bread crumbs. Heat half of the oil in a large skillet. Place tomato slices in the skillet and cook on each side for approximately 2 minutes, or until they are golden brown. After half of the tomatoes are cooked, add the remaining oil and fry the rest of the tomatoes. Drain all tomatoes on a paper towel, then transfer to a cookie sheet and bake at 350°F for 5 minutes. Serve hot with any variety of condiments. Nice accompaniments include a creamy horseradish dressing or a sweet mustard dipping sauce. *Yields 6–8 servings.*

Orange Hush Puppies

No fried seafood dinner would be complete without hush puppies, the wonderfully simple balls of fried dough! They are another Southern specialty, prominent in the Florida Panhandle, that creates perplexing questions for Northern visitors. Although they are simple to make, you'll be lucky to ever find two places where their hush puppies are alike. We hope you will enjoy our zesty orange recipe and compare them to the many other versions you encounter.

2 large eggs	*1/4 teaspoon baking powder*
1 medium Spanish onion,	*1/2 teaspoon baking soda*
chopped	*1 1/2 teaspoons salt*
1 cup whole milk	*1/2 teaspoon crushed black*
2 teaspoons honey	*pepper*
1 teaspoon granulated sugar	*2 cups plain yellow cornmeal*
2 teaspoons orange zest	*1/4 cup all-purpose flour*
1 tablespoon vegetable oil	*Vegetable oil, for frying*

Combine eggs, onion, milk, honey, sugar, orange zest, and 1 tablespoon of vegetable oil together in a mixing bowl. In a separate bowl, sift baking powder, baking soda, salt, pepper, cornmeal, and flour together. Set aside.

Heat half an inch vegetable oil in a large cast iron skillet. The oil is at the right temperature when a droplet of water causes a splatter. If you are cooking with an electric skillet or frydaddy, the oil temperature should be at 325°F. Meanwhile, incorporate the dry ingredients into the milk mixture. Blend well. Drop by teaspoonfuls into hot oil and fry, rolling until all sides are golden brown. Drain on a paper towel and serve with seafood and grits. *Makes 8 servings.*

Conch Fritters

A group of old friends sit on a balcony overlooking the beach, savoring the carefree moment. The beach house screen door opens and someone appears with a tray of icy margaritas and steaming hot conch fritters. These are the Florida moments we cherish and make the grind and hassles of day-to-day life worthwhile. Conch fritters more than any other food represents Key West and the "checking out" perspective that helps us to recharge for the challenges of life. Enjoy these wonderful little bites of heaven as often as you need to.

Fritter

1 cup fresh conch (crayfish make a good substitute if fresh conch is unavailable)
1/2 cup corn nibblets (fresh, canned or frozen corn may be used in this recipe)
2 large eggs
2 cup crumbled stale bread
1 cup fine bread crumbs
2 tablespoons white onion, chopped

2 large cloves garlic, minced
1/4 cup chopped red or green bell pepper
6 dashes Tabasco Sauce®
Juice of 1 large lemon
1 teaspoon salt
1 teaspoon freshly ground black pepper
Vegetable oil, for frying

Batter

1 cup all-purpose flour
1/4 teaspoon salt
2 large eggs
2/3 cup cold whole milk

1 tablespoon extra virgin olive oil
1 dash Tabasco Sauce®

Combine ingredients in order and mix well. Let stand while stuffing mixture is prepared.

Mix all fritter ingredients together into a moist stuffing-like consistency. Form into 1-inch diameter balls. Dip the balls into the frying batter and fry in a pan with half an inch of vegetable oil until all sides have been browned. Drain on a paper towel and serve warm. *Yields 8 appetizer or side dish servings.*

🕭

Thanksgiving Blue Crab Stuffing

This is a holiday favorite, but can be enjoyed year-round. In Florida, our fall bounty comes from both the land (yes, wild turkeys are very much alive and well in Florida) and the sea. A nice dark brown turkey with crabmeat stuffing is a perfect centerpiece to Florida's bountiful harvest. (See p. 95 for super fast, super good turkey.)

1 pound lump blue crab meat

1/2 cup white onion, finely chopped

1/2 cup green pepper, chopped

2 large cloves garlic, minced

1 teaspoon fresh thyme

1 tablespoon fresh Italian parsley, chopped

1/2 cup chicken stock

1/4 cup water

2 cups stale bread, coarsely chopped

1/2 cup celery, chopped

4 tablespoons salted butter, melted

1 large egg, beaten

1 teaspoon salt

1/2 teaspoon pepper

2 dashes hot pepper sauce of your choice

Remove any pieces of shell from crab meat, being careful not to break up the meat as you pick through it. Cook onion, green pepper, garlic, and herbs in melted butter over medium-low heat until tender. Add the chicken stock and water. Stir in the chopped bread. Add the remaining ingredients and mix well. Bake in an oiled casserole dish for twenty minutes at 350°F. Yields 8 servings.

Fresh Mango Salsa

Salsa is a must-have for social events in Florida. The tangy, smoky,
sweetness is a perfect representation of the blends in climate and cul-
ture that is Florida. Why not try making your own as a party show-
case? With the wonderful selection of fresh fruits, peppers, and herbs
available year-round from Florida, salsa can accompany almost any
occasion, and it is easy to make enough for two or for twenty.

2 large cloves garlic, finely
chopped
1 small red onion, diced
1/2 green bell pepper, diced
1/2 red or yellow bell pepper,
diced
1 fresh habanero pepper, finely
chopped
1 large mango

1 medium orange (a large tan-
gerine or small grapefruit
may be substituted)
1/4 cup fresh cilantro, chopped
2 medium limes
2 teaspoons extra virgin olive
oil
Salt and freshly ground pepper
to taste

Combine garlic and onion with all peppers in a large bowl.
Peel the mango and orange and cut into small cubes, being
careful to remove the seeds and center pith. Add the fruit and
chopped cilantro to the bowl, tossing lightly. Squeeze in the
juice of 1 1/2 limes, then add the olive oil, again tossing lightly. Add salt and pepper to taste and refrigerate at least 30 minutes. The other half lime should be cut into wedges and used
as a garnish. *Makes 2 cups of salsa.*

Serve with tortilla chips or other type of corn chip, unsalted
plantain chips, or firm bread. Alternatively, you can use it as
a condiment for fish, pork, or chicken dishes.

❦

Breakfast
Specialties

Fancy Blue Crab Quiche

Quiche is perfect for weekend breakfasts, holidays, or just as a special treat. This is a slightly lighter version than many traditional quiches, adjusted to fit the warmer climate of Florida. Fewer yolks keep the eggs from masking the sweet flavor of the crab meat, and whole milk instead of half-and-half will keep you light on your feet.

Prepared pie crust in a 9-inch deep-dish pie pan
3 large eggs
2 large egg whites
2 cups whole milk
1 cup part-skim mozzarella cheese, grated
1 1/2 cups Swiss cheese, grated
1/4 cup shallots, finely chopped (scallions may be substituted)
1 teaspoon lemon juice

1 tablespoon fresh basil, chopped
1/4 teaspoon ground nutmeg
1/2 teaspoon salt
1/2 teaspoon freshly ground black pepper
1/2 pound blue crab meat, cooked and cleaned (if using pasteurized, pick through meat and pull out any loose shells)

Pierce the bottom of the pie crust with fork several times. Bake at 350°F for 5 minutes, then remove and cool.

In a large mixing bowl beat together the eggs and egg whites. Whisk in milk, and then fold in all the ingredients, adding the crab meat last. Pour the mixture into pie crust. Bake at 375°F for 45–50 minutes, until the top is a golden brown and middle is firmly set. Serve hot. *Makes 6 large or 8 regular servings.*

This dish can be made in advance and frozen up to 2 weeks for a later event. Please note that this quiche should not be reserved only for breakfast or brunch, as it tastes great for dinner as well!

Luscious Shrimp Omelet with Spinach & Cream Cheese

Shrimp omelet with spinach and cream cheese is a decadent breakfast to be served at any time and for any occasion. Whether you have company staying over or want to do something nice for the family, this is a great dish to show off with, while not really having to work very hard. Besides, just about everyone loves an omelet, and why not use the best food Florida has to offer?

4 ounces cream cheese	*3 teaspoons salted butter*
1 tablespoon fresh chives, chopped	*Salt and freshly ground black pepper*
Juice of 1/2 large lemon	*4 large eggs*
1/2 pound fresh medium shrimp, peeled and deveined	*1 tablespoon water*
	1/2 pound fresh spinach, chopped

Mix together cream cheese, chives, and lemon juice. Set aside.

Sauté the shrimp in a saucepan with a teaspoon of butter and salt and pepper for 4 minutes. Remove and set aside.

Cook chopped spinach for 1 minute, drain, and set aside.

Beat eggs and water together and add to a large, hot, well-buttered iron skillet or omelet pan. Cook on medium-low temperature until center begins to set. Layer cream cheese mixture, spinach, and shrimp into the omelet. Slowly pull in the outsides of the omelet to allow uncooked egg to run onto the hot surface. Remove omelet from pan by carefully sliding half of it on to a plate and folding the other half over. *Makes 2 omelets.*

Buttermilk Pancakes with Blueberries & Maple Syrup

For many people, blueberry picking is a fond childhood memory—no exception in Florida, where blueberries happily grow. However, the question always arose after picking: what to do with all those blueberries? Buttermilk pancakes with blueberries and maple syrup was often enough the perfect answer. Every fruit has its best friend: oranges have juice glasses, peaches have cream, and blueberries have pancakes.

1 1/4 cups all-purpose flour
1 teaspoon baking powder
1/2 teaspoon baking soda
1 tablespoon granulated sugar
1/2 teaspoon salt
1 large egg, beaten

1 1/2 cups buttermilk
1/2 pint of fresh blueberries, washed
2 tablespoons vegetable oil
8 teaspoons vegetable oil for cooking

Whisk all ingredients together until smooth. Cook on hot griddle with 1 teaspoon of oil per pancake. Cook until each side has a golden brown color, and serve warm with homemade maple syrup. *Makes 8 5-inch pancakes.*

If your Vermont friends haven't sent you any, here's a substitute:

Maple Syrup
1 cup water
1 cup granulated sugar
2 teaspoons maple extract

Boil water and sugar until all sugar is dissolved and liquid is clear. Stir in maple extract and serve hot or cold over pancakes or French toast.

∽

French Toast with Fresh Strawberries and Bananas

This dish is by no means a Florida exclusive, but bananas are part of south Florida's bounty. When these fruits are in season, you will understand the love we hold for French toast with strawberries and bananas. Having plenty of fruit is key, because it is the star of this recipe. Maple syrup is great accompaniment, but honey or butter alone will work well with fruit.

2 large eggs	*1 pint strawberries, washed*
2 large egg whites	*and sliced*
2 tablespoons milk	*1 large banana, sliced*
1 teaspoon cinnamon	*2 tablespoons powdered sugar*
1 tablespoon butter for frying	*for topping*
8 thick slices of day-old	
French bread	

Beat together eggs, egg whites, milk, and cinnamon. Add a tablespoon of butter to a hot iron skillet or large sauté pan. Dip a piece of bread into the egg mixture, covering both sides but not allowing the bread to become soggy. Add to the hot pan and cook for about 3 minutes each side. Adjust heat as needed in order not to burn the egg mixture. Remove and place on a plate covered with paper towels.

Layer the toast with bananas and strawberries according to your preference. Sprinkle with powdered sugar, serve with syrup on the side, and enjoy! *Makes 4 servings of 2 slices each.*

Mom's Banana Bread

Banana trees are common throughout Florida, although the trees bear the fruit only in the southern half of the state where they are protected from the cold. Bananas plucked straight from the tree seem exotic, yet are also the star ingredient in one of America's great comfort foods: banana bread. This recipe incorporates cream cheese to create a moist loaf that will be loved by all.

1 cup granulated sugar
8 ounces regular cream cheese
2 large eggs
2 medium-size, over-ripe
   bananas, mashed

2 cups all-purpose flour
1 teaspoon baking soda
1 teaspoon baking powder
1 cup broken pecans or wal-
   nuts (optional)

Blend sugar and cream cheese together. Add eggs 1 at a time, beating well after each addition. Incorporate in the bananas, flour, baking soda, and baking powder. Stir well with a fork until combined. Add nuts if desired. Pour batter into a prepared loaf pan (non-stick spray or greased). Bake at 350° F for approximately 50 minutes, until golden brown and a knife comes out clean. Let cool, then slice and enjoy. *Yields 8 servings.*

✤

Sweet Things

Classic Key Lime Pie

This is the classic Florida dessert desired by natives and visitors alike. Until recently, Key lime juice was unavailable outside of Florida. The pies labeled Key lime throughout the United States were nothing more than plain lime juice, green food coloring, and a disputably inauthentic meringue topping. Today, Key lime juice is readily available in grocery stores and at many online grocers. As a result, Key lime flavors are found in such unexpected places as martinis, jellybeans, and fudge. Once you have tasted the original Key Lime Pie, you will understand the Key lime craze and never accept the bright green imposter again.

Graham Cracker Crust
1/3 cup salted butter, melted
1/4 cup granulated sugar
1 1/4 cups graham cracker crumbs

Mix ingredients and press into bottom and sides of a 9-inch, 1.5-inch deep pie plate. Chill for 10 minutes before filling.

Key Lime Filling
1 14-ounce can sweetened condensed milk (the low-fat version
*   also works well)*
4 large pasteurized egg yolks
1/2 cup Key lime juice

Whisk together milk and egg yolks until smooth. Add juice slowly and mix until well blended. Pour into graham cracker crust and refrigerate overnight.* Serve chilled, with a dollop of whipped cream if desired. *Yields 8 servings.*

*If preferred, the pie can be baked at 350°F for 12 minutes. Cool to room temperature and then refrigerate overnight. This is not the traditional method, but is appropriate if you do not want to use raw eggs.

Key Lime Cheesecake

While New York–style cheesecake is always a delicious dessert, a culinary trend in recent years has created unique additions to the original. From pumpkin to huckleberry, cheesecake is now available in almost every flavor imaginable. Key Lime Cheesecake is Florida's contribution to the cheesecake renaissance and ranks high as one of the new innovative desserts in the culinary world.

Graham Cracker Crust
1 cup graham cracker crumbs
1/4 cup granulated sugar
1/3 cup salted butter, melted

Combine ingredients and press down into bottom of a 9-inch springform pan. Bake at 325°F until the crust is set and golden, approximately 8 minutes. Chill for 10 minutes.

Cheesecake Filling

1 cup Key lime juice
1/4 cup water
2 1/4-ounce unflavored gelatin packets
1 1/2 cups granulated sugar
4 large pasteurized eggs, beaten
16 ounces cream cheese, softened

1/2 cup salted butter, softened
1/2 cup heavy whipping cream
1 tablespoon grated Key lime peel
Sliced Key limes, for garnish

On stovetop, combine Key lime juice and water. Add gelatin and let stand for 5 minutes to soften. Blend in sugar and eggs and, over medium heat, slowly bring to a boil. At boiling point, remove from heat and continue to stir for 1 minute. Beat cream cheese and butter in medium bowl. Slowly pour in hot Key lime juice mixture and beat at medium speed until well blended and smooth. Refrigerate until cool. Beat whipping cream until stiff peaks form. Fold into Key lime mixture along with Key lime peel. Pour into chilled crust and refrigerate for 4 hours. Serve chilled, garnished with whipped cream and Key lime slices.

If you prefer to cook it, bake for 10 minutes at 350°F, until the filling has set. Cool on a wire rack, then refrigerate. *Yields 8 servings.*

ᴄᴈᴢᴐ

Fast and Fancy Angel Food Cake with Chocolate and Strawberry Sauce

This dish was inspired by a great meal that was lacking a dessert. An angel food cake, seasonal fruit in the refrigerator, and a candy bar later, a popular and easy dessert was born. It is quick, light, and refreshing. In addition, your guests will think you spent a long time in its preparation. Because of light texture and rich flavors it matches well with most Florida cuisine, whether you are having a spring evening feast or an Indian summer barbeque.

1 pint strawberries (raspber-
ries can be substituted)
1 tablespoon granulated sugar
2 tablespoons orange juice
1 pound dark chocolate
1/4 cup heavy cream

1 standard-size angel food
cake, sliced into 1 1/2-inch
wedges
Fresh mint for garnish

In a saucepan, combine fruit, sugar, and orange juice, and simmer for 10 minutes. Remove from heat and blend with a hand blender or mash with a potato masher in the saucepan. Set aside.

In a small double boiler, slowly melt the chocolate. As the chocolate melts, stir in the cream until a thick, smooth liquid is formed.

To serve, spoon approximately 2 tablespoon of the chocolate sauce onto dessert plate. Place angel food cake wedge in center of the plate, then drizzle with fruit sauce. Serve with a sprig of fresh mint. *Yields 10 servings.*

Note: A close friend of ours used this recipe as the inspiration for her wedding cake. While she used a classic New York–style cheesecake instead of angel food cake, the spirit of the dish held true. It was a nice compliment.

Tres Leches (Three Milk Cake)

This popular Latin dish can be found at Spanish and Cuban restaurants throughout Florida. Once you have prepared it for yourself, you'll easily understand why. The three milks used in preparing the special syrup create a luscious richness that will not soon be forgotten, and the cool cake will make a wonderful finale for any Latin-inspired meal or as a light treat.

5 large eggs
1 cup granulated sugar
1 1/2 teaspoons plus 1 table-
    spoon vanilla extract
1 cup all-purpose flour
1 14-ounce can sweetened con-
    densed milk

1 12-ounce can evaporated
    milk
1 cup whole milk
3 large egg whites for frosting

Grease a 13 x 9 x 2-inch baking pan with cooking spray or butter.

Separate 5 eggs. Beat the whites in a large mixing bowl on medium speed for 3 minutes. Continue to beat eggs, while slowly adding 1 cup of sugar to the bowl. Add the yolks one at a time, beating after each addition. Stir in 1/2 teaspoon of vanilla extract. Add flour to the egg mixture until combined, being careful not to over-mix. Pour into prepared pan and bake at 350°F for 20 minutes, until the cake pulls away from the sides of the pan. Cool completely, and then prick the whole cake with a fork.

Blend the 3 milks with 1 tablespoon of vanilla extract. Pour the syrup over the cooled cake, covering completely.

Beat 3 egg whites to soft peaks. Gradually add 1 cup of sugar and beat until stiff peaks form. Stir in 1 teaspoon of vanilla. Transfer to a small pot and cook over low heat, stirring constantly, just until sugar crystals dissolve. Remove from heat and continue to stir until cool. Frost cake with the meringue mixture.

Refrigerate for at least 1 hour before serving. *Yields 10–12 servings.*

Tallahassee Lassie Pecan Tassies

Tallahassee Lassie Pecan Tassies are a fun substitute for a traditional pecan pie at the holidays and also make a great Christmas cookie. They are like mini pecan pies, a single burst of nutty, gooey, crunchy yummi-ness. When you make them, you'd better make a lot of them. Then just sit back and watch the smiles appear as the tassies disappear!

Pastry Crust
3 ounces cream cheese, softened
1/2 cup sweet cream butter
1 cup sifted all-purpose flour

Blend ingredients together and chill for 1 hour. Shape into 1-inch balls and press dough against bottom and sides of mini muffin pan. Chill in the refrigerator for 30 minutes.

Pecan Filling
Beat egg and blend with all ingredients except the pecans

1 large egg	*Dash of salt*
3/4 cup dark brown sugar	*2/3 cup pecans, broken into*
1 tablespoon salted butter,	*medium-size pieces*
softened	
1 teaspoon vanilla extract	

until smooth. Add pecans and stir. Fill tart shells 2/3 full. Bake at 350°F for 25 minutes until filling is set. Cool and then remove from pans. *Makes 18 tartlets.*

⊂✥⊃

Tangy Lemon Bars

Lemony and delicious, these bars are perfect for a picnic or garden party, as well as for an afternoon snack with a tall glass of sweet tea. This tasty, sticky little dessert may also be made in cold weather to go with a mild afternoon or evening cup of coffee or tea. Our recipe is so simple you can have them available for all occasions if you so desire.

Crust
1 cup all-purpose flour
1/2 cup unsalted butter
1/4 cup confectioners sugar

Blend together and spread into bottom of a 13 x 9 x 2-inch baking pan. Bake at 350°F for 20 minutes.

Lemon Topping
Beat eggs and lemon juice together. Add in sugar, baking pow-

2 large eggs   *1/2 teaspoon baking powder*
2 tablespoons lemon juice   *3 tablespoons all-purpose*
1 cup granulated sugar   *flour*

der, and flour. Pour over crust and bake for 20 minutes more at 325°F. After 10 minutes, cover with foil and finish cooking. Cut right away and sprinkle with confectioner's sugar. *Makes 24 bars.*

∽

Southern-style Pecan Pralines

Pralines represent the Deep South and thus are more common in the Florida Panhandle than in central and south Florida. Memories of that first bite of warm, sugary goodness inspire smiles from all that experience this rich dessert candy. Pralines are wonderful with coffee after a meal or as a treat for kids taking a break from summer adventures.

2 tablespoons salted butter
2 1/3 cups packed light brown sugar
1/4 cup water
2 cups broken pecans

With a wooden spoon combine butter, sugar, and water in thick-bottomed pan over medium-low heat. Once sugar has dissolved, cook for 5 minutes longer, stirring continuously. Add pecans and stir for approximately 4 minutes.

Remove pan from stove. Place spoonfuls of the mixture onto waxed paper. Cool at room temperature for 1 hour and then remove by peeling back waxed paper underneath the pralines. Store in an airtight container for up to 2 weeks. Yields 10–12 servings.

Blackberry Tart

Blackberry season occurs in late summer. Lucky people have wild bush-es near their houses. The ambitious ones venture forth to woods near and far to fill their buckets (and mouths!) with these tart berries. Others simply recognize the season and pick up a pint at the local farm-ers' market. No matter what your method of acquisition, we encourage you to enjoy the berries while they are in season. Fresh blackberries can be served with yogurt, whipped cream, zabaglione, or highlighted as the star attraction in the tart below.

Pastry dough

1 1/2 cup all-purpose flour
*1 1/8 sticks cold unsalted but-
ter, cut into half-inch
pieces*
1/4 cup sugar

1/2 teaspoon salt
1/2 teaspoon fresh orange zest
2 large egg yolks

Combine flour, butter, sugar, salt, and orange zest in a food processor and process until mixture forms a coarse meal. Add egg yolks and process just until they are incorporated and the mixture begins to clump.

Turn mixture out onto a work surface and divide into 2 portions. With floured fingertips, press the first portion into the bottom of an 11 x 1-inch round tart pan with a removable bottom to form a quarter-inch-thick crust. Use second portion to form sides of crust, also a quarter-inch thick, and mold up to the top of the tart rim. Chill for 30 minutes.

Filling

Stir sugar, cornstarch, and nutmeg together in a large bowl.

1/2 cup granulated sugar
1 1/2 tablespoons cornstarch
1/4 teaspoon nutmeg
*1 1/2 pints fresh blackberries
(blueberries can be substituted)*

1 tablespoon fresh lemon juice

Add blackberries and lemon juice and toss gently with a fork, making sure to coat all the berries. Let mixture stand, stirring occasionally, for 30 minutes.

Preheat oven to 425°F. Arrange filling in pastry shell, overlapping in a rosette pattern. Pour all juices from bowl over the blackberries.

Bake tart uncovered in the middle of the oven at 425°F for 15 minutes, then reduce temperature to 375°F. Cover tart loosely with foil and bake until blackberries are tender and juices are bubbling and slightly thickened, 40–45 minutes more. Remove from oven and place on a rack while still in pan. The juices will continue to thicken as the tart cools. Once it is cooled completely, carefully remove the pan rim from the tart. Slice and serve with fresh mint for garnish. *Yields 10 servings.*

Mamma Guava Pastry

In addition to the usual scones, muffins, and croissants in Tampa's coffee shops and bakeries, guava pastries are abundant. There are usually two varieties of the pastry: guava and guava with cream cheese. Both are simply delicious, especially with café con leche—think of it as paying homage to Tampa history!

*8 ounces cream cheese, at
    room temperature
2 teaspoons granulated sugar
1 pound puff pastry
2 tablespoons salted butter,
    melted*

*1 17.5-ounce container of
    guava paste
1 large egg
1 teaspoon water
1 tablespoon unrefined cane
    sugar*

Blend cream cheese and white sugar in a small bowl. Set aside. Slice puff pastry lengthwise, making columns approximately 3 1/2 inches wide. Brush each side of pastry with melted butter. Liberally spread guava paste over strip of pastry. Spread 1/8 of the cream cheese mixture on a second strip of pastry. Lay the second strip over the first, in a sandwich style, with cream cheese and guava paste together inside the pastry. Beat egg and water together and then brush the top of the pastry lightly. Sprinkle with a bit of the unrefined cane sugar. Slice the column into 4 pieces and place on a cooking sheet lined with parchment paper. Repeat with the remaining ingredients until complete. Bake pastry in a 350°F oven for approximately 10 minutes, or until the tops are lightly browned. *Makes 16 pastries.*

Note: Guava paste is available in Hispanic groceries or online at specialty food sites.

ᵒᴥ᷽

Condiments

All-the-Time Mustard
Yogurt Sauce

This cool dipping sauce is very easy to make, and it is this simplicity in preparation, not to mention the decadent taste, that makes this dipping sauce so special. The spicy wine-infused flavor of Dijon mustard is a natural compliment to the creamy smooth texture and slightly sour flavor of the yogurt. A little heat and texture from whole-grain mustard and you have a veritable masterpiece.

1 tablespoon Dijon mustard
1 teaspoon whole-grain mustard
1/2 cup plain low-fat yogurt (mayonnaise can be substituted)
2 dashes hot pepper sauce of your choice

1/2 teaspoon fresh dill, finely chopped
Salt and fresh ground black pepper to taste

Mix all ingredients together and cool in the refrigerator for at least 15 minutes. This sauce can be used on any meat and most fish and shellfish. It can be a base for salad dressings or vegetable dips. The possibilities are endless. *Makes 1/2 cup.*

❧

Voodoo Sauce

Hot sauce is a natural accompaniment to many Florida specialties: oysters, po' boys, blackened grouper, crab cakes, and jambalaya to name a few. While there is an abundance of hot sauces of various flavors and intensities on the commercial market, it can be very rewarding to make your own. Our first attempt was a result of a habanero pepper plant gone wild. With no guidance except the ingredient list on one of our favorite brands, we embarked on a three-hour adventure. Some of our discoveries include the following:

1. *A gas mask comes in handy as the habanero peppers are cooking. If no gas mask is available, a clean cooking towel will serve just as well to shield your nose and mouth from the burning fumes.*
2. *Good ventilation helps, whether it is an open door or window, the stove fan, or both.*
3. *An immersion blender saves the hassle of transferring ingredients from the cooking pot to a blender, and saves fingers from coming in direct contact with the burning peppers.*
4. *As we have never met anyone who likes to serve hot sauce out of a large mason jar, have lots of small bottles ready to transfer the finished product into. A turkey baster can aid in the transfer when the bottle opening is narrow.*

Keep several bottles for yourself, but distribute the rest to your heat-loving family and friends. For a fun touch, put warning labels on the bottles warning consumers to have milk on hand during consumption.

2 large cloves garlic, diced
*2 large carrots, coarsely
    chopped*
*1 medium red onion, coarsely
    chopped*
*1 pound habanero peppers
    with stems removed*

1 cup white vinegar
1 cup water
1 tablespoon salt
1 teaspoon granulated sugar

In a large pot, cook the garlic, carrots, and onion together for approximately 10 minutes. Add the peppers, vinegar, water, and salt. Cook over high heat until boiling. Add the sugar and reduce to a simmer. Cover and cook for 30 minutes. Blend until smooth using an immersion blender, or if you prefer, blend after transferring the ingredients to a food processor or blender. Return ingredients to the pot and continue cooking for another 30 minutes, then repeat the mixing process. Simmer for 1 additional hour, then let cool.

This sauce can be bottled or frozen. It will last indefinitely in the refrigerator. Share it with your family and friends, warning them that this is a very hot sauce with voodoo qualities. *Makes 4 cups.*

⬲

Kickin' Cocktail Sauce

No seafood table can be complete without the quintessential red cocktail sauce. Whether you use it for crabs, fish, shrimp, oysters, or any other seafood, you should always have it fresh and available in large amounts. (Some people will use copious portions.) The version we settled on and have used for years is the preferred style with our family and friends: hot, zesty, and kickin'!

1/2 cup ketchup
1/2 cup horseradish sauce (not
   creamy-style)
1 tablespoon fresh lemon juice

3 teaspoons hot pepper sauce
   of your choice

Mix all ingredients together and serve. The sauce is usable for about 4 days when stored in the refrigerator. You can also add your favorite fresh herbs or hot peppers for a fun alternative. *Makes 1 cup.*

Index

A
alligator, 59
anchovy, 48, 52
Apalachicola, 39, 40
avocado, 54

B
bananas, 25, 111, 112
beans, 57, 59
beef, 90, 92, 94
bisque, 56
blackberries, 25, 122-123
blackening spice, 64
bloody Mary, 29
blueberries, 25, 110
bread, 112
burger, 90
butter, drawn, 68, 69
buttermilk, 110

C
Caesar salad, 52
Cajun, 62, 63, 68, 86
cake, 117, 118
catfish, 85
Cedar Key, 56
cheese, blue, 90
cheese, cheddar, 99
cheese, cream, 33, 109, 112, 115,
    119, 124
cheese, feta, 36, 48
cheese, Monterey jack, 99
cheese, mozzarella, 60, 108
cheese, parmesan, 34, 41, 42, 52,
    74, 76, 78, 82, 89
cheese, ricotta, 82
cheese, Swiss, 66, 108
cheesecake, 115
chili, 59
Christmas, 119
chocolate, 117

cilantro, 44, 46, 51, 54, 71, 81,
    106
citrus, 37, 46
Clamato, 29
clams, 76–77, 78
cocktail, 36, 39, 129
coconut, 92
coconut cream, 30
coffee, 24
cole slaw, 80
conch, 103
cornmeal, 102
Costa Rica, 44, 71
crab, blue, 42, 54, 56, 69, 84,
    105, 108
crab, soft-shell, 63, 80
crab, stone, 54, 68
crackers, 35, 39
cream, heavy whipping, 41, 74,
    115, 117
Creole, 86
croutons, 52
Cuba, 5, 7, 24, 28, 66, 118

D
dip, 33, 34, 106

E
eggs, 108, 109
evaporated milk, 24

F
fish, 44, 64, 70, 71, 72, 85
French toast, 111
fritter, 103
fruit smoothie, 25

G
Gainesville, 23
garlic, 71
Greek, 48, 90

grapefruit, 46
grits, 86, 98-100
grouper, 44, 64, 70, 71
guava, 124

H
half-and-half, 37, 56
heart of palm, 34, 36
horseradish, 39, 129
hot sauce, 29, 39, 62, 66, 86, 99,
    127, 103, 105, 127, 129
hush puppies, 70, 102

J
Jacksonville, 1
jambalaya, 86

K
Key lime juice, 114, 115
Key limes, 114
Key West, 13, 14, 30, 64, 103

L
lamb, 90
lemon juice, 24, 27, 37, 53, 71,
    72, 89, 94, 108, 109, 120
lemons, 24, 27, 50, 53, 62, 71, 72,
    89, 94, 95, 109
lime juice, 27, 31, 44, 46, 79
limes, 31, 44, 46, 79, 106
lobster, 54, 82

M
mango, 25, 44, 79, 106
maple syrup, 110, 111
margarita, 31
marinade, 94
Miami, 11–13
milk, evaporated, 24, 118
milk, sweetened condensed, 114,
    118

mint, 23, 27, 117
mushrooms, 42, 96
mussels, 37
mustard, 65, 85, 126

O
Old Bay Seasoning, 65, 69
omelet, 109
onion, 57, 60, 102
orange juice, 26, 37, 41, 70, 72,
    79, 117
oranges, 37, 44, 46, 72, 79, 102,
    106, 122
Orlando, 11
oysters, 39, 40, 58

P
Panama City, 64
pancakes, 110
Panhandle, 10, 85
papaya, 51
pasta, 74, 76, 78, 82
pastry, 124
pecan, 112, 119, 121
Pensacola, 1
pepper, bell, 44, 46, 59, 86, 103,
    106
pepper, chili, 57, 59, 76, 78, 86
pepper, habanero, 44, 46, 79,
    106, 127
pepper, jalapeño, 86, 99
pie, 114
pineapple juice, 30
pizza, 88
po' boy, 62, 63
pork, 65, 79
potato salad, 48-49
pralines, 121

Q
quiche, 108

R
roll, 64
rum, dark, 28
rum, Jamaican, 30
rum, light, 26, 27

S
sage, 82
salad, 48, 51, 52, 54
salsa, 44, 106
salt, sea, 72
sandwich, 62, 63, 64, 66
sauce, 78, 126, 127, 129
sausage, 57, 66, 86
scallops, 33, 44, 74, 86
seafood, 33, 37, 39, 40, 42, 44,
    50, 54, 56, 58, 62, 63, 64, 68,
    69, 70, 71, 72, 74, 76, 78, 80,
    82, 84, 85, 86, 88, 103, 105,
    108, 109
shrimp, 33, 44, 50, 62, 74, 86, 88,
    109
snapper, 72
soup, 57, 60
spinach, 41, 109
Spring Hill, 29
St. Augustine, 4
St. Petersburg, 48
stew, 58, 92
strawberries, 25, 26, 111, 117
stuffing, 105
sugarcane, 27, 92

T
Tallahassee, 5, 11, 119
Tampa, 5, 7, 37, 57, 66, 124
tangerine, 46
Tarpon Springs, 48, 90

tart, 122
tea, iced, 23, 99
tequila, gold, 31, 44
Thanksgiving, 105
tomato, 48, 51, 59, 64, 66, 74, 75,
    78, 86, 96, 101
turkey, 95

V
Vidalia onions, 60
vodka, 29, 127

Y
Ybor City, 5, 57
yogurt, 25, 50, 64, 65, 92, 94, 126

If you enjoyed reading this book, here are some other Pineapple Press titles you might enjoy as well. To request our complete catalog or to place an order, write to Pineapple Press, P.O. Box 3889, Sarasota, Florida 34230, or call 1-800-PINEAPL (746-3275). Or visit our website at www.pineapplepress.com.

The Essential Catfish Cookbook by Janet Cope and Shannon Harper. Mouthwatering recipes that call for succulent catfish and a variety of easy-to-find ingredients. Learn about the private life of the captivating catfish and enjoy this Southern delicacy. (pb)

Exotic Foods: A Kitchen & Garden Guide by Marian Van Atta. Grow avocado, mango, carambola, guava, kiwi, pomegranate, and other rare delights in your subtropical backyard. Includes planting and growing instructions as well as over one hundred recipes for enjoying your bountiful crops. (pb)

Mastering the Art of Florida Seafood by Lonnie T. Lynch. Includes tips on purchasing, preparing, and serving fish and shellfish—with alligators thrown in for good measure. Also includes instructions for artistic food placement, food painting techniques, and more. (pb)

The Mongo Mango Cookbook by Cynthia Thuma. Much more than a book of easy-to-make recipes, this book is also a compendium of mango history, legend, and literature. It traces the fragrant fruit's genesis and its proliferation throughout the world's warm climates, and explains why the mango's versatility and palate-pleasing flavor make it a favorite among chefs. (pb)

The Mostly Mullet Cookbook by George "Grif" Griffin. Mulletheads unite! Includes dozens of mullet main dishes, such as Dixie Fried Mullet, Mullet Italiano, Sweet & Sour Mullet, and the Sea Dog Sandwich, as well as mullet-friendly sides and sauces and other great Southern seafood, including Judy's Mullet Butter and Ybor City Street Vendor's Crab Cakes. (pb)

The Storm Gourmet by Daphne Nikolopoulos. When the power goes out, most people find themselves unprepared—especially in the kitchen. This book includes shopping lists for creating an emergency pantry; more than 70 recipes; menus for quick, well-balanced meals; a guide to growing fresh herbs inside; and advice about weathering the storm. (pb)

The Sunshine State Cookbook by George S. Fichter. Delicious ways to enjoy the familiar and exotic fruits and vegetables that abound in Florida all year round. Includes seafood cooking tips and delectable recipes such as Rummed Pineapple Flambé and Caribbean Curried Lobster. (pb)